Finding Shirley:
The Jim Esala Story

By Susan Stanich

29th Avenue Press

Finding Shirley:
The story of Jim Esala
by Susan Stanich

Printed in the United States of America

ISBN 978-1-60266-464-7

Bible quotations are taken from the King James Version Standard Text edition, Cambridge University Press, © 1995.

Chapter heading quotations are from:

The Meditations of the Emperor Marcus Aurelius Antonius, translated by George Long. New York: A.L. Burt Company.

The Imitation of Christ by Thomas á Kempis, translated by Richard Challoner. B.F. Laslett & Co., 1910.

Young India, editorial by Mohandas Gandhi, Sept. 25, 1924, in Volume XXV of *Collected Works.*

Lame Deer Seeker of Visions, by John Fire Lame Deer and Richard Erdoes. New York, 1972: Simon & Schuster Pocket Books.

White Roots of Peace by Paul Wallace, Leon Shenandoah foreword. Santa Fe, 1994: Clear Light Publishers.

Remembering Mother Theresa, *The Passionists Compassion,* Winter 1997, Vol. 51.

Interview with Desmond Tutu, *Around for You: Understanding Yourself and Others,* Feb. 6, 2007.

The Divine Comedy by Dante Alighieri. Translated by Stephen Mitchell. In *The Enlightened Heart.* New York, 1989: Harper and Row.

New Seeds of Contemplation by Thomas Merton. Norfolk: New Directions, 1972.

Daylight by J. Rumi. Translated by Camille and Kabir Helminski. Monterey, CA: Threshold Books, 1995.

Marian Wright Edelman, Selected Quotations, from *About Women's History,* New York Times Co., 2007.

Note to Reader

With two exceptions, all the main characters and most of the minor characters in this book are (or were) real people. Some names have been changed, however - most notably, that of Shirley Johnson. As publication date neared, her family members realized they were not quite ready to go public about this very idiosyncratic woman, even though they did want her story to be told; changing her name seemed the best solution.

The two exceptions mentioned above are Douglas (the Vietnam veteran) and Reino Mikkonen.

Although Douglas himself is a fictionalized composite of many people in Jim's life, the record of the conversation is real. In addition, the conversion and the offer of gasoline all actually happened, many times, in many places, with many people.

The completely fictional Reino walked into these pages uninvited. "Hey!" he said forcefully. "You can't go writing about all this stuff Jim and his friends believe without giving another side of it. A lot of people around here don't agree with it, you know; it's not fair to leave us out."

He was so insistent, he finally got his way.

Dedication

To Don Hanson, butcher and theologian, who with his friend Jim personifies what true Christianity can be;

To Jim's prayer partners and friends, who were determined that this book should come about;

To Jim's family, with thanks and hopes this book hasn't been too much of an intrusion into their lives;

To the Ruis family of rural Elk River, Minnesota;

And most of all, to Jim -

This book is dedicated.

A man like this carries within himself a whole heart, a universal heart, from which others of his era have somehow been torn, as though by a blast of wind.

- Fyodor Dostoyevsky

Foreword

A friend of a friend called one day and asked if I would consider writing a book about a born-again Christian, an unusually kind older man who lived in a community not far from my own.

I had met born-again "Christians" before. With a few exceptions, I didn't much like them. I didn't mind that they took scripture literally; for us puny-brained earthlings, that's probably the best way to remember and understand the larger and more universal messages behind them. What I did mind was that many born-agains seemed self-righteous, authoritarian, hypocritical, judgmental, rigid, small-minded and coercive. Many of the whites among them were racist and anti-Semitic as well. Plus, what the born-agains called their "love" always seemed to have a string attached - their idea of what others should be, and if the others didn't fall into line, the love evaporated. Besides, like many of their main-stream Christian brethren, they appeared to know how to make their religion into a private money-making endeavor. They seemed to believe that their wealth was proof that God loved them; the pursuit of wealth, in their minds, was intertwined with the pursuit of Truth.

I told him I was pretty busy.

Then the caller added that Jim Esala had devoted his life to helping others, and he received no remuneration for it. He just went out and helped people - *no strings attached.* Jim himself had no money, and the people he helped were usually the kind of people that society had rejected.

A born-again Christian with genuine compassion? Sensing that he had my attention, the caller asked if I would come to a barbecue, where Jim and his prayer partners would be, and just meet him and think about it. Jim wasn't being told about the book plan.

The scene was a roomy deck overlooking a thoughtfully landscaped yard at the edge of a forest in Cloquet, Minnesota. About eight men were there. The huge steaks were grilled perfectly, the corn-on-the-cob was sweet and tender. But Jim wasn't there.

His friends explained that he had been detained; his mother-in-law was disabled, and Jim and his wife were giving her 24-hour care.

We visited for about an hour, during which time I decided I would not do the book. Then Jim arrived. I was struck immediately by his gentlemanly but humble bearing. He looked strong for a man of 76 and was quiet spoken. In the conversation that followed, I noticed that his language seemed to be the very language of love. Its flow went right through him, as though he were of no importance whatever, and out to the rest of us.

During the following months, I learned a great deal about Jim Esala, and about his kind of Christianity.

Jim is a true believer - an old-fashioned born-again evangelical. But he's an inclusive, rather than exclusive sort of believer. He doesn't judge people, leaving that up to God.

Instead, he simply loves people - no strings attached.

Contents

One of the greatest diseases is to be nobody to anybody.

- Mother Teresa

PROLOGUE

Shirley

Shirley's head throbbed. She tried to open her eyes, but something was keeping one of them shut. She touched it. Her fingers met a painful swelling that reminded her: that man. She glanced at the form lying in the bed next to her, and tried to remember his face. The guy who had hit her. Even with his back to her, she could smell the mixture of alcohol fumes and bad breath his huge snores were exhaling.

Who the hell was he? Where was she? It was very dark. Trying not to jostle the bed, she slowly slid her bare legs over the edge and sat upright. The floor was dirty and cold to her feet. Squinting, she examined the scene beyond the second-floor window. Lights from the street revealed a familiar brick building across the street. Superior. She was in Superior, Wisconsin. She had come with this guy, whoever he was, and the bastard had got what he wanted from her and then slugged her for some reason or other. But she hadn't got hers yet, only four drinks, and he had promised her a whole bottle. Damn cheapskate.

She stood unsteadily, waited until the dizziness abated, and moved carefully through the dark room to the table and picked up the bottle. It was empty, but she drained a few drops and found her cigarettes and lit one. Standing there, balancing herself against the table – damn place didn't even have a chair – she tried to collect her thoughts.

But her thoughts wouldn't take form. Boozy distorted images floated through her mind: *The missing bottle. Her husband (where did he go last night, anyway?). Their little boy (a quick tinge of guilt; she banished it. He was probably okay by himself, he could manage, he was probably at home asleep). This cheapskate in the bed there – she still couldn't conjure up his face. Christmas…it was tomorrow, or maybe yesterday. Her Valium.*

Her Valium. Shirley felt around the table, but couldn't find her purse. She knelt on the floor and crept around the table until she found the purse, upended, her things spilled out. But the Valium bottle was there. She took two, swallowing them dry. Then her hand brushed something hard. It was another bottle – not even opened yet. As she gratefully stripped away the tax stamp, she shot a glance of appreciation toward the sleeping form. "Here's to you, honey," she toasted him, as she took a long swig.

*   *   *   *   *

The phone shrilled into the night at the Esala home, awaking Jim and his mother, Elizabeth. It was 3:30. The dawn of a northern winter was hours away.

"Hello?"

There was breathing on the phone, and finally a woman's slurred voice: "Hey. Come get me."

"Shirley? Where are you?"

"I dunno. Somewhere in Superior. I think on Tower. Across from that old movie house, maybe."

"Are you all right?"

"I dunno. Jus' come. 'Bye." She hung up.

*   *   *

"Picking up Shirley" had become routine with the Esalas. The routine started with the search - to find which bar or flophouse she was in, whether in Cloquet or Duluth, or across the Lake Superior bay in Wisconsin. There was often a struggle to get her into the car. It ended with Shirley sound asleep in Elizabeth's bed.

Tonight, it had taken the Esalas two hours just to find her, and she had forgotten she had called them. She fought being taken away from "my sweet man. You goddamn do-gooders, you jus' leave me an' my honey alone!" She fought as they got her coat onto her, Jim fending off the angry man. They wrestled her into Jim's car, where she promptly threw up. They drove to their house along Big Lake Road, and Elizabeth cleaned Shirley up as Jim cleaned the car before the vomit froze to the seat and floor. Elizabeth bedded Shirley down in her own bed, where Shirley threw up again.

Now Shirley was clean once more and sleeping soundly between fresh sheets, and Jim and his mother were having coffee in the kitchen. They didn't waste words wondering who the man was, or where Shirley's husband was. This was old stuff with Shirley and Roger Johnson. They didn't discuss how hard this life was for the little Johnson boy, who thankfully was safe at a neighbor's house. Later they would take Shirley to her home on the other side of town.

They prayed for Shirley, and for Roger, and for little Kenny.

> *Jim did that for years. Over and over and over again, he'd pick Mom up, she'd swear at him, throw up, all of that mess - she'd sober up, and then a couple of weeks later give him another call in the dead of night. He just wouldn't give up.*
> *- Ken Johnson, Minnesota businessman*

Bruised children. Neglected babies. Disconnected teenagers, broken fathers and mothers, lonely single adults.

Alcoholism, drug abuse, sex tourism, materialism, child pornography. Greed, hatred, jealousy, suspicion, disrespect, bullying.

Triple-locked doors, attack dogs, drive-by shootings, road rage.

A litter of used drug syringes in the alleys, used condoms on the beaches, unused land mines awaiting the feet of children. Puddles of industrial waste and methamphetamine poisons.

Regardless of whether we're rich or poor, or who we backed for president; regardless of our religion or sexual orientation or ethnicity; we can agree that our world would be better without this misery. We might not like one another's choices and lifestyles. We might even be totally opposed to them. But most of us want a world where we are kind to our children and to our neighbors, where a strange face doesn't arouse fear, where vulnerable people are safe, where we can enjoy the night sky without worrying that we might get clubbed or robbed. When we put aside our skepticism and cynicism, our outrage and resentments, most of us know, deep down, that what we really want is a world of love.

This is the story of a small-town Midwesterner who has helped others all his life, by simply and humbly extending love and trust to them. He would be the last person to think he was special. He just does what he feels he is called to do. He sees goodness and promise in everyone. His story gives us hope.

*Time is like a river made up of the events
which happen, and a violent stream; for as soon as
a thing has been seen, it is carried away,
and another comes in its place, and this will be
carried away too.*

-Marcus Aurelius

CHAPTER 1

Early Childhood

The story starts in Cloquet (rhymes with croquet), a lumber town in northeastern Minnesota. The time was Valentine's Day, 1928, less than 10 years after a devastating fire swept through the region and killed 450 people. Some townspeople were still in shock and grief, including Elizabeth Esala. The sight of the burned bodies of her friends continued to haunt her, vividly and terrifyingly, and now she was burdened with a fresh sadness as well: Her baby was coming and her husband hadn't returned home. It was already 11 p.m.; if Walfred was up to his usual tricks, he was drinking somewhere and wouldn't be back for a day or two. That morning she had deposited two-year-old Bud with her mother and stepfather on their farm five miles away. Now the labor pains were getting stronger, the snow was falling even harder, and she needed a ride to the hospital.

"Lily!" she called the young woman who was staying with them temporarily while looking for work.

It took only a few minutes for Lily's sleepy face to appear. "Yah, Mrs. Esala?"

"The baby's coming!" Her voice became a gasp as another contraction flooded her. "Go wake up Mr. Soulier and see if he can drive me to the hospital!" The snow was too deep for cars, but the neighbors down the street had a good team of horses and a sleigh. Looking frightened, but saying nothing, Lily pulled on a coat and boots, wrapped her head in a scarf and disappeared into the snowy darkness. Elizabeth leaned over until a contraction passed.

Lily was with her at the Epperd Hospital when, the following morning, the boy she would call Jim was born. He came into the world on the tail end of the Roaring Twenties, a period of economic boom that culminated the following year with the bust of the Great Depression. Jim's family and most of his neighbors weren't much affected by either the boom or the bust. His neighbors - Swedish, Finnish, Ojibway, French-Ojibway - were mostly poor. They farmed, gardened, hunted, logged, found odd jobs, fished…and they got by.

*   *   *

Bud was wary of his new baby brother, who stole their mother's cuddly milk time. The boys' father was wary because, although he liked kids, he wasn't sure he wanted to be tied down with another one. Elizabeth's stepfather, Frank Pitts, was wary because he didn't want to be stuck somehow with another mouth to feed, a kid who wasn't even his blood grandchild - and he didn't like kids anyhow. The other set of grandparents, the Esalas who lived nearby, weren't involved with the young family.

Only Elizabeth and her mother welcomed Jim with open hearts. They admired his size, his sturdy intelligence and his easygoing personality. They prayed for his health and long life, and that he would become a good Christian.

It was the women who did the praying in the Esala extended family. Jim's mother and grandmother were practicing "saved" Christians; his father and step-grandfather were practiced scoffers. The split produced strife, and a personal animosity between the two men caused even more problems. Jim became attached to Bud, and from the time he could walk, followed him everywhere.

He loved Bud. Bud was big and the best of everybody. *Someday, I will be six too and big like Bud.*

But one day Bud was gone. Jim's father was mad. Jim could hear him yelling. He ducked behind a chair and peeped out.

"You mean she just walked in here and took him?" Dad yelled. Mom was crying. "Yes, you know how she - how she is, she -"

"I damn well do know! So do you! Why didn't you stop her?"

"I - She said that we have Jim, so Bud can live with her and Frank, and then she packed his things and took him."

"And you just stood there! I suppose that damn Frank helped her, too."

"No - well, he was waiting in the truck - "

Dad stomped out the door and slammed it. When Dad did that, he wouldn't be back until tomorrow. Maybe he was going to Grandma's and Gramps' to get Bud and bring him back home. But Jim didn't think so. He started crying.

*   *   *

It was two weeks before Jim saw Bud again. Grandma brought him along when she delivered the basket of laundry for Elizabeth to wash in the electric washer; Grandma and Gramps had no electricity. Teary-eyed, Elizabeth hugged her eldest son so hard he began struggling to get free. Grandma explained that one reason she had taken Bud was that Elizabeth wasn't in good health and didn't have the strength to raise two boys.

"But Mama, I -"

Grandma raised her hand authoritatively, silencing her daughter.

10

"For another thing…"

Jim stopped listening, because Bud had finally escaped his mother's arms.

"C'mon outside, Bud!" Jim whispered joyfully, "Come see what I got!"

They slipped out the door. Jim ran around the house and returned pulling a new red wagon. Uncle Wilho had pasted a Phillips 66 emblem on it.

"Hey, this is nice!" Bud said. "Where'd you get it?"

"Dad got it. Wanna try her out?" Jim was in seventh heaven. First Bud pulled him, and then he pulled Bud, and then they found a little grade and went down it together. The front wheels skewed around and they were dumped out in the grass. They were in a giggling fit when a horn sounded. Jim hadn't even noticed the Model T truck parked right there on Larch Street in front of the house. Gramps was waiting in it. He honked again.

When Grandma and Gramps drove away, Bud securely between them, Jim ran after the truck a little way. It disappeared onto Big Lake Road and he sadly turned back to his house. Mom was standing at the front door, crying.

*   *   *

Jim's mother had been born in Sweden. Grandma - Ida Romlin - had brought her to the United States when she was tiny. What became of Grandma's husband in Sweden was never explained; she married twice more after bringing her 11-year-old daughter to Cloquet. The first American husband died, leaving Grandma his farm and log house. The second was an English immigrant, Frank Pitts, who moved onto the place.

Frank was Jim's "Gramps."

The next time Gramps pulled his Model T pickup in front of the Esala home, he came alone. He disappeared into the house with a laundry basket. Jim crept under the canvas truck box cover and hid there in the dark. He heard Gramps come back out; heard his footsteps to the truck; heard them pause. Then the canvas was thrown back, and there was Gramps, looking down at him impatiently.

"What you think you're doing?" a gruff voice said.

"I wanna see Bud...."

Gramps lifted Jim out and dropped him on the grass. Jim's little black-and-white dog, unaware that she had given away her small owner's hiding place, licked his face. Gramps drove away without saying another word. Jim tried several more times to stow away, but Gramps always caught him.

For the rest of Jim's childhood, Bud's home was with Grandma and Gramps on their farm. He came back for occasional lengthy visits, and Jim visited the farm for long stays too, but the brothers would not call the same place home for another decade.

They also attended different schools. Jim went to Leach School, just two blocks from home. A family friend, Mrs. Christopherson, had made him a rug for his nap there, but he never used it; he was 5 years old now, and too grown-up for a nap. Lois and Rosella, who walked to school with him, did take naps. *Girls can,* Jim thought. *Big boys don't. Bud doesn't.*

One morning on the way to school, a cloud of grasshoppers flew up in front of them as they cut across the grass. He dropped his lunch pail and chased up some more.

"Stop it, Jimmy!" Rosella screeched. "They're getting in my face!"

There really were a lot of grasshoppers. Some of them wouldn't even move when he charged through them. They were too busy eating. He couldn't help walking on some. They squished and crackled under his feet.

"Ohhhh, icky!" wailed Lois.

When they got to school, their teacher, Miss Johnson, explained that there was a grasshopper plague. It wasn't so bad here, but in Northwestern Minnesota, they had eaten every last green thing.

"Even the corn?"

"Yes."

"Even the birch leaves?"

"Yes. Everything. They even ate fence posts."

"Even green sweaters?" asked Lois, who was wearing one.

"Well, no; they eat vegetation. You know, plants, and…some wood."

"Is it all brown there now?"

"That's what they say."

"Will it get all brown here too?"

It already was kind of brown; several years of drought were taking their toll on the trees and crops.

13

"We hope not," Miss Johnson replied. "The farmers are spreading poison for them now."

Sure enough, when Jim and his mother visited Grandma and Bud on the farm, Bud led him to the shed and pointed out gunny sacks of poison stacked neatly there. Jim saw big letters stamped on the sacks: U-S-D-A.

"What does that spell, Bud?"

Bud pointed at each of the four letters, his eyebrows puckered in thought. "It spells 'the government.' The government brought those sacks."

"What do you do with them?"

"Play on them. C'mon!"

They were jumping on and off the sacks, raising powdery clouds through the burlap, when Gramps found them.

"Hey, you kids, get off of them sacks!" he shouted. "That stuff is poison! Where's your brains?"

They got down. Gramps left.

"What's poison, Bud?"

"It's kind of like medicine."

"My teacher said they're feeding it to grasshoppers. Are the grasshoppers sick?"

"I guess so."

The next day, Gramps and other farmers mixed the arsenic with molasses and bran, and hauled it away in wagons to spread it on their fields. The grasshoppers never did arrive in massive numbers, however, and even where the bait wasn't spread, the drought-dried plants survived. Some people said the bait killed more deer and cows than it did grasshoppers.

*   *   *

The Esalas lived where the city of Cloquet had spread into the Fond du Lac Reservation. Julius Coffee lived nearer the center of the reservation, several miles beyond Cloquet. He was selling his cabin and 15 acres for $400. Jim's father borrowed the money and bought the place.

On moving day, Jim watched wide-eyed from the car as they pulled off Big Lake Road and up to the Coffee home. There was a wonderful fragrance in the air: fresh-cut jack pine. The odor made it seem special. Mainly, the rickety new home was special because it was two miles closer to Bud. Near the house was a shed, which soon became home to a cow (Margaret) and some chickens. Next to the house were an outdoor pump and a mountain ash, the only tree on the place.

"I don't want you planting trees and flowers all over, like you did at the other house," Dad warned Mom.

But it wasn't long before Mom had flowers and Norway pines planted everywhere. Then Dad growled that she'd better not water them; with the continuing drought, the well would go dry. Determined to have beauty around her, she waited until he was at work at Northwest Paper Company in Cloquet before hauling water from the well to nourish the struggling young plants.

Northwest Paper was making its fine paper famous with commissioned illustrations of stalwart, red-uniformed Mounties in the great outdoors. The ad campaign had begun two years earlier, and became one of the most successful ad campaigns in history, eventually commissioning hundreds of paintings for calendars, posters and greeting cards.

Jim's father was a crane operator at Northwest, but he wasn't noble like the Mountie who represented the company. Increasingly, he was coming home drunk, and when he got drunk he got mean, even violent. He minded his manners when there was a guest in the house, however, and often some bachelor in need of a place to hang his hat bunked in the little room upstairs, which was accessible by a steep outdoors stairway. Mom valued these guests, for they were her unwitting protectors.

One winter day after school, as darkness was descending, Jim burst into the house anticipating fresh homemade buns and jam. Instead, he found the kitchen walls smeared with jams and jellies, and smashed glass on the floor. It looked like every last jar of Mom's canned preserves had been thrown against the walls. He heard someone upstairs. The most recent guest had moved out two days ago.

Jim went upstairs and cautiously pushed open the door. There was Mom, with all of Dad's guns and what looked like every last knife in the house. She turned to him, looking determined and a little panicky. "Quick, son, help me hide these things before he comes back," she gasped. They put the weapons under the mattress.

A car door slammed. "Shhh," Mom whispered, her finger to her lips, her eyes wide. Footsteps sounded downstairs; then there was no sound; then they were coming up the steep stairway. Mom set herself to block the door. Jim leaned against it too. His heartbeat was battering his eardrums.

He felt a push from the other side, and heard a growl from Dad: "Open the damn door!"

They said nothing.

Dad got louder; he was swearing. Then with a big shove, he thrust the door in.

He took one look at mom and roared, "I'm going to kill you!" He grabbed her around the throat with his big hands. She was backing up and gagging. Jim pushed in between his parents, screaming; the terror in his voice seemed to get through to Dad. Dad dropped his hands and stepped back, panting and blinking as though confused.

Even though Jim's world seemed to be exploding, an odd calm came over him, and a thought came into his mind, as clear as well water: *Someday I'm going to be big enough to manhandle my dad.*

*   *   *

Every Sunday, Grandma and Mom took the boys to Sunday school at Zion Lutheran Church in town, where Pastor O.L. Nelson had baptized the boys together. Jim liked Sundays, because he could see Bud, and because they would ride in Grandma's Whippet car. Grandma had bought it with money sent by wealthy relatives in Sweden. Pastor Nelson said the Whippet was named after a dog that was small and fast. He said that at an all-day race in Indiana between a lot of different kinds of automobiles, the Whippet was one of the fastest.

After church one warm, sunny morning, Grandma and Mom stopped on the steps to visit with several women. Bud was playing on the lawn with some older boys. Jim had his chance. He climbed into the Whippet and got behind the steering wheel.

He moved the wheel back and forth, making a motor sound: "Mrrrrrrrr." He examined the wheel. It had a button on it. Pastor Nelson said that button was one of the things special about a Whippet. Jim played with it a little. It moved. He clicked it clockwise and waited for something to happen. Nothing did, as far as he could see, but Grandma must have seen something, because she looked over at the car and went straight as a stick, like she was scared or mad. He turned the button back, and pushed it. The horn blasted, and he jumped; Grandma was really barreling over to the car now. He pulled the button out, and the engine started. Wow! He was reaching for the gear stick when Grandma opened the door and ordered him out.

She said nothing to him on the ride back to the farm for Sunday dinner. Mom said nothing either; she deferred to her strong-willed mother in most matters. There was a dinner guest, as usual; both Grandma and Mom were always inviting strangers or one of the many bachelors in the area to dinner. This time it was John Hoaglund, who had brought along some good-smelling bread that he baked himself. Jim picked up a slice and examined it. John kept his log cabin neat and clean, unlike most of the bachelors' places Jim had seen. Jim wouldn't eat anything from some of those places, but this bread looked good. He spread it with some of Grandma's wild plum jam. Then he helped himself to pot roast with onions, boiled cabbage, potatoes mashed with rutabagas, and cooked carrots. He tried not to look at Grandma.

After everyone had finished their yellow cake, Grandma told Jim to come into the kitchen. Grandma was tiny, only four feet tall, but she had a strong way about her that made people pay attention. Jim watched her as she silently washed and wiped her prize platter. She handed it to him and motioned to the top shelf. He stepped up on the stool and carefully slid the blue-trimmed platter onto the shelf. He jumped down. Grandma looked at him hard.

"Jim, that button on the steering wheel is the finger-tip control," she said. "It turns on the lights and makes the horn go. It also turns on the automobile, and that could be dangerous. You don't want to do that again, because you might get hurt."

He did want to, though, and after that he climbed into the Whippet's driver's seat every chance he got.

*   *   *

Dad decided to build a new house. The house would have a rock-concrete foundation and be built with bricks made in nearby Wrenshall. Jim helped the delivery man unload them from his dump truck. The bricks weren't rough and red, like some bricks Jim had seen; these were smooth, almost soft, and of a creamy pink-rust color. The man had a strong

Finnish accent and said his name was Prince Albert. Jim liked him. After the second load was piled near the foundation, Prince Albert leaned on the truck, lit a cigarette and looked down at Jim.

"You know, I could have been your father," he said.

What? A different father? For a moment, Jim imagined how that would be - a dad who didn't attack Mom and didn't get drunk and spoil the jam. Maybe this man really was his father, and the grownups had got mixed up. Feeling half hopeful, half guilty for betraying Dad with his hope, he ran into the house and told her what Prince Albert had said.

Mom just chuckled. "No, son," she said. "You're such a fine boy, he maybe wishes you could have been his. But what he said isn't true."

Jim was partly relieved, and partly disappointed.

The house was finished in late November. They moved in just ahead of the first heavy snowfall. It was a fine house, with three rooms and a bathroom downstairs and two bedrooms under the slanted roof upstairs. They got hooked up to a new electric line that came from the University of Minnesota Forestry station on the other side of the reservation, across Otter Creek and then down the Swanson Road that bordered their property.

Soon familiar radio voices sounded again in the Esala home: "It's a beautiful day in Chicago!" exclaimed the cheerful host of the National Farm and Home Hour. "Oxydol's own - Ma Perkins!" declared the soap opera announcer as an electric organ whined that era's version of mall music. "The Lone Ranger rides again!" proclaimed a heroic voice to the background clatter of running hooves.

Because theirs was the first home on the reservation to get electricity, the head of Minnesota Power and Light called to wish them a Merry Christmas.

Christmas! With the excitement of moving into the new house, Jim had forgotten all about it. Then he had a worried thought: They probably were going to Grandma's for the holiday; how would Santa Claus to be able to find him? He decided to make a sign:

SANTA CLAUS WE ARE THIS WAY FROM JIM ESALA ▶

On Christmas Eve, which Grandma and Mom called *Julafton*, they were dressed and ready to go, bowls of food and cookies already packed in Dad's 1929 Chev with the disc wheels. Dad was in a good mood, and Jim went outdoors with him to start the car and warm it up. When Dad was feeling good, Jim liked being around him and helping him.

It was already dark, and stars were bright in the cold clear sky. The insides of Jim's nostrils got frosty, and the dry snow under his boots squeaked. When Dad pushed the starter, the engine made a low groaning sound and wouldn't turn over. Jim turned to get his sled; obviously they were going to have to walk to Grandma's, and they'd need the sled to haul the packages.

"Where are you going, Pootie?" Dad asked as he got out of the car. Dad called him "Pootie" sometimes when he was in a good mood. Dad's breath made steam clouds in the air that picked up the light coming from the kitchen window.

"I'm getting my sled."

Dad chuckled. "Good thinking, Pootie. But I don't think we'll need it. I'll show you a little trick to get 'er going."

Dad got a metal pan and started a fire in it with a half-dozen slender-split sticks of dry oak. When the wood had burned down to coals, he slid the pan under the crank case.

"It's got to be coals, and no flames, or else the rubber hoses and fittings could burn," Dad explained. "The coals will warm the crankcase and thaw the oil." Sure enough, after a half hour the engine turned over, and they were on their way.

Grandma's house looked warm and welcoming in the dark. Bud was waiting impatiently for them in the chilly entryway. "Come inside and see the tree, Jim!" he exclaimed, and led the way into the living room, where a decorated balsam stood. Its fragrance filled the room. When Gramps lit the candles, the room seemed enchanted.

The holiday was wonderful. Jim and Bud got presents - clothes and toy cars. They had lutefisk, which Gramps as usual refused to eat; ham and meat-balls; potatoes and hardtack; cabbage and pickled herring; rice pudding. They could have Christmas pastries any time they wanted. Dad's good mood lasted all through Christmas. He even joined them for *Julotta*, the early morning candlelight service at Zion Lutheran, and he visited pleasantly with the preacher later. Gramps stayed home.

*   *   *

The following spring, Mom seemed to be sick a lot. During her spells, she sent Jim to Grandma's. He walked into Grandma's kitchen one day just as one of her coffee-drinking neighbor ladies, Mrs. Murphy, was leaving, and another, Mrs. Skunk, was arriving.

Mrs. Murphy was Irish and came from Alabama and talked funny. She had a hard life with her mean husband and many children. Their cabin was back in the woods a way; Jim had been there and seen the dirt floor, and how their beds were right on the cold ground. Grandma felt sorry for her.

Mrs. Skunk was Indian and from Fond du Lac. Jim didn't know if her husband was mean or whether they had dirt floors. She settled into the chair just vacated by Mrs. Murphy. Grandma went out to the summer kitchen to fetch hot coffee, and returned with more cake. She handed Jim a piece and sat down to visit with Mrs. Skunk. Jim remained, standing near the visitor, leaning over her and sniffing. Grandma shot him a sharp look. "Run along, now," she told him.

Bud wasn't around. Jim went out to the pile of sand and toy cars he and Bud played with. Gramps spotted him playing.

"Doing nothing like a lazy lad, and the barn needs cleaning," he said sourly.

Jim kept moving his truck back and forth.

"Well?" Gramps asked threateningly. "I need help in there."

Jim didn't move. He hated working with Gramps, who got mad a lot and sometimes smelled like beer, same as Dad.

"You heard me! Get yourself into the barn!"

Jim jumped to his feet. "I don't hafta! You're not my real grandpa anyhow!"

Gramps started after him. Jim ran for the house; in the entryway he almost crashed into Mrs. Skunk, who was coming out of the kitchen. She nodded at him on her way out, but he kept on going, until he was safe behind Grandma.

Gramps came in mad. Grandma plucked a stick of wood from woodbox and held the weapon high, a fiery look in her eyes. "What's going on here?"

Even though Gramps towered over Grandma, he always seemed to wilt when she faced him down. He explained what Jim had said, and Grandma put the wood down, but she turned her fiery look on Jim. "Do as you're told," she said sternly. "That barn needs cleaning."

Grandma was back in the summer kitchen when Jim finished. Grandma didn't use the regular kitchen in the summer time, because the house would get too hot. The summer kitchen was stifling from the wood cook stove, and Grandma's face was red.

"Grandma, why doesn't Mrs. Skunk smell bad?" he asked.

"Oh-ho, is that why you were sniffing around her?" Grandma erupted. "Clump Jack!" She whacked him on the shoulder. It was a friendly whack; none of the four adults ever hit or spanked the kids.

"Well, skunks smell bad. But she doesn't."

"Oh Jim, that's just her name, a regular Indian name. Don't you never do that again. It's not polite." Then, as an afterthought, she asked, "Why did you say Gramps isn't your real grandfather?"

Jim picked at a piece of bread on the table. "I dunno. I just said it."

Back at home, he and his friend Leo Rabideaux were returning in the dusk after playing in Otter Creek. They stopped suddenly when a skunk, followed by her three babies, crossed the path. Jim was reminded of Mrs. Skunk and Indian names. Leo was Indian.

"Leo, does your name mean 'skunk'?" he asked.

"I don't think so. Does yours?"

Jim giggled. "No, it means weasel."

"No, it means rat!" Leo crowed.

"No, it means grasshop—Hey! What about Mrs. Grasshopper?"

He never thought about it before; Mrs. Grasshopper's name. She visited Grandma too, and he never wondered whether she could hop. He guessed that names were just names.

"Leo Mosquito!"

"Jim Horsefly!"

He never did think to ask Grandma what "Clump Jack" meant.

The following Sunday in the Whippet, Grandma told Mom they were switching churches. From now on, she said, they were going to Bethany Evangelical Covenant Church. That suited Mom just fine; she had been saved at age 10, through the efforts of a Salvation Army marching band in Minneapolis, and the Lutherans didn't seem to have the same zeal as the street missionaries. Grandma and Mom liked the new church and its preacher, Arnold Tamte.

At Sunday dinner, Grandma told Gramps they had changed churches. "Oh, is that so," he said; it was of no interest to him. Then he gave Mom a hard look. "Where's that no-good husband of yours, out drinking again?"

Jim's stomach churned. Dad said the same thing about Gramps. He wished they could like each other and not be mad so much. He and Bud slipped away from the table to play outside.

Later Gramps called them to evening chores. The boys got the cows in from the pasture and washed their udders. Jim's hands weren't strong enough yet to milk a cow dry, but he could start one, and Gramps would finish. Jim balanced on the barn stool and leaned his forehead against the warm flank. Gramps didn't name his cows. This one was an easy milker, and her teats were just the right size for his hands. He liked the sound the milk made as it hit the clean pail. First it pinged, and then, as the milk level rose, it made a thick swishy-gurgly sound. The barn cats gathered, anticipating their pans of warm milk. Jim tipped a teat and shot a stream of milk at a cat. She didn't seem to mind the milk in her face; she even opened her mouth a little.

When Gramps had a full pail, he set it up high on the feed bin in the adjoining horse barn, where his team, Morgan and Florry, stayed in cold weather. Then he blew back the foam and took a drink. *Yecccchh,* Jim gagged at the sight. He didn't like milk - unless it was made into the Finnish-Swedish soured milk that seemed to have so many names: *filabunk, viilia, long milk, fil mjölk, tete mjölk, viili-bema.* Grandma always had some filabunk in a jar, either on the counter, or sunk in the coolness of the well if it was hot out. She would spoon some out into serving dishes, and then add more fresh milk to the starter that remained, and the next day it would be ready to eat again. The rubbery filabunk tasted tangy-good, and it was fun to eat. When Jim took a spoonful and lifted the spoon high, the milk held together in a long stretching line, and then the mass below pulled the spoonful back into the bowl, leaving the spoon as clean as if it had just been washed. And it was fun to suck the thick milk through his teeth. Jim especially liked the filabunk from the top of the jar, which was mostly cream if he got to it before Grandma stirred it up. Often Grandma made filabunk from skimmed milk, though, and then it wasn't so thick and rubbery. Grandma sold most of the cream to the creamery.

Bud and Jim each carried a pail of milk into the entryway, where Grandma had the cream separator ready. Jim's Sunday trousers were damp from spilled milk, but he felt proud that he had been able to carry that heavy pail all the way to the house with only one rest and three small spills from the pail bumping against his legs. He and Bud poured the milk into the separator's top bowl and took turns turning the crank. The cream came out of one spout, and the skim milk out of another.

That chore done, Bud went to get the slop bucket.

"I'll help you, Bud!" He grabbed one side of the handle. Both boys were big for their ages, and together they carried the large bucket easily. They took it out to the ditch by the driveway and dumped it.

"You're getting pretty strong, Jim," Bud told him.

Jim suppressed the joyful grin that was about to escape him, and instead made his voice as deep as he could: "I'll take care of the water."

He got a clean bucket, went to the pump, and filled it with fresh water. Bud helped him bring it into the house and pour it in the crock. Then the brothers went out to fetch wood for the cook stove, so Grandma could have it ready in the morning to cook breakfast.

Dusk had fallen, and mist rose in the lowlands. They paused to breathe in the moist, sweet-smelling air and watch the fireflies beginning to sparkle in the growing darkness. The land was hushed and peaceful.

"I like this," Jim said. Then he thought a moment about beauty and how it got made, and he added, "God's nice."

Mosquitoes made them hurry. They dumped their armloads of wood into the woodbox, and Mom said it was time to go.

*   *   *

A terrible thing had happened. Long Johnson, a bachelor whose log cabin was behind Grandma's house, had been beaten to death.

"Oh, that poor old man!" Grandma wailed. "Who could have done such a terrible thing?" The sheriff couldn't find the perpetrator.

Bud and Jim cut back across the meadow and through the woods to inspect the murder scene. Long Johnson's place had a shed with a birch bark roof and a very old log cabin. Through a broken window, the boys could see that the murderer, or somebody, had torn up the inside. The whole place seemed empty and silent. There was a small swamp near the cabin that had quite a bit of water in it, despite the continuing drought. The water in the middle of the swamp was very still, as though Long Johnson had taken away the air when he died. It felt spooky there.

By the time deep winter had settled, the murderer still hadn't been found. Remembering the swamp, the boys went back to Long Johnson's carrying ice skates and a shovel. They cleared a perfect little skating rink, built a fire to keep warm by, and skated until dark.

Grandma was mad when she learned where they had been. "That killer might be around still! You stay away from that place!"

Of course, that made Long Johnson's even more alluring. Bud outmaneuvered Grandma by setting his trap line in such a way it went past the dead man's cabin. Now, when Grandma asked where they were going, he told her truthfully that they were checking the snares. Jim hoped they could snare a murderer, but mostly they got rabbits. That winter there were so many cottontails and snowshoes that dozens of popple trees along the way had been girdled by sharp rabbit teeth. They found blisters on the skin of many of the rabbits they skinned, and they had to throw the carcasses away because those rabbits could make you sick. Occasionally they got a weasel. Jim didn't like skinning weasels; they smelled bad.

One Saturday, Jim was following Bud along the trap line through fluffy snow that had fallen the night before. Bud carried his .22 as usual; he was a good shot. He was watching the trail for tracks and up ahead for movement in the woods. He was silent. Suddenly he stopped, bent under a snow-heavy spruce branch and said something in a low voice.

Jim stepped off the trail and came up beside him, bumping the branch and dislodging the snow onto Bud's head and shoulders. "What did you say?" he asked in a loud, clear voice. There was a rustle ahead; a deer bounded away.

Bud stood up and wiped the snow from his bare neck. "You got to be quiet in the woods, Jim, or you never get to see anything," he said calmly.

Bud never got mad at him. They never fought or even argued, and they divided everything equally. Grandma sometimes gave them a little money so they could buy a treat at Landstrom's store. Sometimes they would buy a pint of ice cream, and sit in the ditch by the side of the road and eat it before it melted. Or they might buy a small sack of mixed candy. Bud would parcel out the pieces: one for Jim, one for himself, one for Jim, one for himself....If there was one piece left over, Bud cut it in careful halves. Jim really liked those Tootsie Rolls.

*   *   *

Grandma liked the Covenant church so much that she wanted a midweek meeting too. So she arranged to use Long Johnson's old cabin for a Thursday evening meeting place, and Pastor Tamte agreed to lead the meetings.

By now the cabin was being claimed by weeds, moss and small creatures. It was as though nature itself was forgetting the murder. Mom and Grandma took brooms and scrub pails and cleaned the cabin as well as they could. Pastor Tamte convinced Dad to help him build some wooden benches, hauling the materials by way of the shortest trail, which led about 150 yards from the Big Lake Road to the cabin. By midsummer it was ready.

The evening was hot and mosquitoes came in swarms from the marshes. Grandma told Bud and Jim to start green-hay smudges in tin cans, and to keep them going. The smoke seemed almost as bad as the mosquitoes. Seven people came. As darkness fell, an old gas lantern was lit, and moths joined the smoke and mosquitoes.

After Pastor Tamte started the service, Jim saw something through the smoke that he thought at first was a trick of the flickering lantern. One of the walls seemed to be moving. He poked Bud in the ribs and motioned toward it. Bud saw it too. Pretending to replenish a smudge, they moved around toward the wall and put their hands against it. Something was moving there - not the wall itself, but something inside. Fear shot through Jim, raising the hair on his arms. Maybe it was Long Johnson's killer, hiding in there. Or maybe Long Johnson himself, still alive, playing a trick on everybody. Or - dread thought - what if it was his ghost, mad that they were using his cabin?

By now several adults had seen it too; Pastor Tamte stopped preaching in mid-sentence. Slowly, warily, one man approached the wall. He opened a pocket knife and quickly slashed the felt-paper wall covering - and leaped back in horror. A writhing garter snake fell out, and the lantern illuminated a mass of shiny squirming blackness still in the wall. There were lots of snakes.

It took a couple of moments for everyone to get over the shock and make sense out of what they were seeing. The explanation was simple: snake pairs were nesting and raising their live-born young between the weather-loosened paper and the walls.

Pastor Tamte broke into the silence with a loud sigh. "Well! The Lord makes his presence known in many ways!" He chuckled. "I guess we won't have to worry about mice in our new chapel!"

Jim liked the preacher. Dad seemed to like him too, and began attending both church and chapel, to the great pleasure of Mom and Grandma.

When winter came, the meetings became more difficult. It was up to Bud and Jim to spend Thursday afternoons preparing for the evening service. They beat a trail through the snowy woods, sometimes using skis, from the road to the chapel. They started a fire with pieces of birch bark that had fallen from the shed roof, and wood they gathered or hauled in on the long trail.

It was rare that more than seven or eight people attended the Thursday services, but Grandma had an iron will and insisted the little group persevere. Spirit, not size, was what counted, she said.

In the beginning, Jim followed the service in his usual way, which was to sing and pray when the grownups did, and try not to fidget or giggle when they were looking.

But one evening, he noticed something: When everyone sang together, it felt really nice; it was something special. The feeling grew, until the specialness filled the room and made him feel like he was glowing inside. He felt his eyes fill with tears, but he didn't feel sad; it was because everything was so beautiful. When Pastor Tamte made the altar call, Jim went forward, knelt down, and invited Jesus into his life.

Shirley

On January 29, 1936, the O'Neill family of rural Carlton in northern Minnesota welcomed its sixth and last child: Shirley, small and ruddy, freckle-faced and lively. Her closest sibling was five years old when she was born. The one who would be her favorite, James, was 14. The farm family was Roman Catholic - loving, tolerant, and abstinent.

A man at his best is like flowing water. Water benefits all things and does not strive for anything. It flows into low places that others disdain.

- Lao Tzu

CHAPTER 2

Commitment

Leap forward 70 years. Jim, now white-haired but still straight and strong, is brewing coffee.

"Hell-oooo-oh!" a sweet voice calls from a back room.

"How are you doing, June? You want to get up?" Jim calls back. "We got something good for you: the coffee's on."

"Oh goodie! *I love coffee, I love tea…*" the sweet voice croons the 1940s Ink Spots' song.

The house is small, neat, old-fashioned. Sunshine floods the living room and brightens the kitchen, which seems too small for Jim, who at 76 still towers over most men. But his every move is thoughtful, "in the present," as he sets cups and saucers on the table.

"I love the java java, it loves me…"

Jim disappears into the back room to help the owner of the sweet voice - June, 86, frail in mind and body - out of bed.

This is my first meeting with him since agreeing to do this book. I am a little wary, hoping I haven't made a mistake. What if it turns out he is a real crackpot? Or just another small-minded bigot? But so far, so good...

June is Jim's mother-in-law, and this is her home, nestled in the woods in Sawyer. In the yard, I had passed through a world of color: a dozen or more large pots of blooming flowers. This has to be Jim's work, for he was a florist for many years. He is here because June's heart is giving out; she spends more and more time in bed and needs full time care; and he and Chery, his wife of 24 years, have virtually moved in. Today Chery is at work in Duluth, and Jim has the watch.

"Coffee and tea, the java and me...." Right on the beat.

June appears in the kitchen, a smiling ray of sunshine in a light cotton housecoat. Jim walks beside her, holding her up. His hold is discreet, protective of her modesty, but as stable as a rock. It's clear that she trusts him completely.

Her smile and song are infectious, and I join her singing the next line: *"A cuppa cuppa cuppa cuppa - coffee!"* Her shoulders make a slight rhythmic wiggle with each *"cuppa,"* and she laughs wholeheartedly. Her joyful beauty gladdens my heart.

Jim helps her into a comfortable chair by the table. He's courteous and gentle with her. Her eyes light up when she sees the cup, and after introductions and a brief chat, she focuses on her coffee as Jim and I talk.

I ask him about Shirley Johnson. I'm particularly interested in her story, because her son Ken is my friend. I've often wondered how he not only survived his nightmarish childhood, but was able to become a family man, raise healthy, sociable children and run a successful business.

Jim thinks for a moment before answering.

"Shirley was a blessing," he says.

I almost choke on my coffee. A blessing? She and her husband drank and caroused and neglected their small son to the point of abuse. Many nights they never bothered to come home, and the frightened little boy slept with a knife under his bed. At age 10, he was already driving them around: his panic-struck mother to Moose Lake State Hospital; and his father to a bar in nearby Wisconsin, where bars were open on Sundays, to drink away his delirium tremens. If it hadn't been for neighboring families, and for Jim and Jim's mother, Ken would have had no parenting at all.

"Whoops! Mr. Moto, I'm a coffee pot." June knows all the verses. She smiles at me; she can tell that the song is running through my head too, and that I also like it.

"Shirley was honest," Jim explains. "She'd tell it like it is. She was honest even though she had a terrible time with her demons."

I nod, thinking he's speaking of metaphorical demons. Ken had told me about his mother's panic attacks and her long struggle with addictions - alcohol and tobacco, some drugs.

Jim continues. "She and Roger used to come down to our storefront mission in Cloquet, at 120 Avenue C. Like many of those who came, they often came drunk."

He shifts in his chair and puts up his large hand. "Let me back up. My mother and I first met the Johnsons at a home on Big Lake. We went there to visit, and Shirley and her husband Roger happened to be there. Everybody there was drinking, I mean heavy. The man who lived there - he was a pretty tough character - he introduced me as a 'preacher.' Right away, Shirley shot us a mad look. She was a redhead, you know, a small woman, and she was a little firecracker. Her eyes just flashed. 'I'm a *Catholic!*' she said. 'Don't you try converting *me!*'

"Well, I wasn't one to go around trying to convert people, and neither was my mother. You've got to respect people, you know. You just go to give them love, not to change them.

"Anyway, Shirley and Roger started coming in to the mission. They just came and sat, maybe learned some scripture - they didn't reach out and really receive Christ. But we got better acquainted, and sometimes Shirley would get stuck someplace in the middle of the night and call and have us pick her up."

"Ken told me about that," I put in. "He said you did that over and over again -dozens of times."

Jim chuckles. "It wasn't always easy, because she had that hot temper - we had a hole in the door where she flung a butcher knife through it.

"Anyway, very early one morning, it was about 3 o'clock, on our way home after one of the rescue trips down in Superior, Shirley said she wanted to go the mission. When we got there, my mother and I tried to be quiet because there were renters upstairs, and they were asleep. Of course that didn't bother Shirley at all; she turned the volume up. She was still very drunk.

"She knelt down at that old makeshift altar we had and started doing her rosary. My mother was standing beside her, praying with her. She had her hand on Shirley's shoulder.

"After a little while I just took authority over the demon of alcohol and cast it out in Jesus' name. And Shirley flipped right over backwards on that hardwood floor. I'd never seen anything like it before. She'd been on her knees, and then her body flipped right over, I mean *hard*, like she'd been thrown. She lay there on her back, and couldn't move; she was paralyzed from the waist down. My mother was worried. I told her to kneel down and put her hand on Shirley's chest and pray for her, which she did. Then Shirley started screeching - well, it wasn't Shirley, it was the demons coming out of her making those terrible screeches. When they stopped, her paralysis was gone and she could get up. She was delivered from all the demon forces, and she was completely sober.

"That was her deliverance. It cleaned up her morals, her vocabulary; and, as far as I know, she never drank or smoked again."

I am completely silent, trying to take it all in. *Real demons*, I think. *He's talking about real demons...*

Well, what difference does it make? What does "real" mean, anyhow? One way or the other, Shirley

Johnson had been in the grip of something stronger than herself, something terrible that was destroying her life. And then she was free from that grip. Ken had told me that his mother became a helpful and productive person for the rest of her life, and she never used alcohol or tobacco again.

"Ken said you saved her," I say. "The way he put it was, 'Jim reached down into the depths of hell with his strong right arm and pulled my mother out.'"

Jim shakes his head. "The Lord did that. All I did was to be obedient, to do His will. I saw Shirley as the Lord sees her: complete and perfect."

Jim rises, selects a large glass from the shelf, and fills it with cool water. He sets it in front of June like the precious thing it is. "You know what, June?" he says. His voice, I realize, has been cheerful and free from care this whole time. "Water is a wonderful thing. It's a healer. It will help you get well. The more you drink today, the better you'll feel tomorrow."

June thanks him and takes a sip. She looks longingly at her empty coffee cup. For her health's sake, Jim and Chery try to restrict her coffee; but Jim catches the yearning look and pours her another half cup.

"Waiter, waiter, percolator," she sings with a smile.

I don't preach a social gospel; I preach the Gospel, period. The gospel of our Lord Jesus Christ is concerned for the whole person. When people were hungry, Jesus didn't say, "Now is that political or social?" He said, "I feed you." Because the good news to a hungry person is bread.

- Desmond Tutu

CHAPTER 3

Growing Up

J im gazed dismally at the long row of young carrots that stretched out in front of him in the hot sun. It looked like it went on forever. Bud was already partway down his row, moving slowly along on his knees, thinning the carrots. Jim sighed, knelt down and started pulling out some tiny plants to make room for others to grow. After this row was done, there would be more rows - carrots and then rutabagas. Gramps' truck garden was huge. Most of his income came from the produce he sold to boarding houses and private homes in the area.

A shadow fell over him, and a foot nudged his knee.

"You're taking too many," Gramps said. "And make sure the one you leave is tight in the ground."

Jim seethed. It wouldn't be so bad if Gramps paid them the way he promised. Every day they wrote their hours on the calendar, but they never saw any money. Then Jim remembered that he was a Christian now, and should be tolerant and forgiving. It sure was hard to be that way around Gramps, though. He wondered if Grandma had told Gramps that he had received the Lord. He hoped not. Gramps sneered at things like that.

He thought of a conversation he had overheard during haying last August. Gramps had been raking hay with the mare, Florry, and was swearing in front of his hired men about how hot it was.

After Gramps had passed by, and the sounds of jangling harness traces and the squeaking rake receded, Joe Diver leaned on his fork and wiped away the sweat on his face. Joe was the best hay man around, Gramps always said, even if he was the son of a chief. Joe had taught Jim how to cock hay - to fork it into perfect haystacks that could repel the rain.

"You'd think he'd be happy with this good haying weather," Joe said as he watched Gramps and Florry maneuver a turn at the far end of the field.

"Nah," Pete Olson responded. "That man curses the sun because it's too hot, and he curses the rain because it's too wet, and he curses the snow because it's too deep. I never saw anyone curse so much."

"Probably curses the moon too, when nobody's looking," Joe chuckled. Then he noticed Jim and shut up.

As he thinned carrots, Jim tried to see it from Gramps' point of view. Last year was the hottest summer ever, and a lot of Gramps' vegetables dried up; so much hard work went for nothing. Then came the coldest winter ever - 50 below on Jim's birthday. An early calf died, and the rutabagas Gramps kept for wintertime cattle feed had frozen despite their thick insulation of soil and hay. So Gramps had a reason to be bad-tempered.

Jim paused and examined a small carrot. *Ooops. I should have left that one in...* The hired men had been right, though. Gramps cursed whether the weather was good or bad, whether a calf died or grew healthy. Jim thought that Gramps probably cursed all of God's creation. There would be some sense to it if it made Gramps happy; but Gramps was never happy. Grandma said he would be happy if he received the Lord.

What did that mean exactly, anyway - "receiving the Lord?" Jim felt like it meant getting soft inside, and letting Jesus make all the decisions for you after that, and not worrying about what might happen later. But how could he always know what Jesus decided? For instance, what if it seemed like Jesus didn't want him to thin carrots - maybe the Lord didn't want all those baby carrots killed - should he stop doing it and not worry about the grownups getting mad? He tried to hear Jesus' voice directing him to save the carrots, but he didn't have any luck.

Jim and Bud thinned vegetables for a week. They worked alongside one another on parallel rows, and they reached the ends of their final rows together. At last! Now for a swim in the creek … But here came Gramps, carrying two hoes. They wilted in disappointment.

Gramps was telling them where to hoe when Grandma came into the garden. "That's enough," she called as she came toward them quickly, stepping across the rows. "These boys have been working hard and now they need some fun."

"Fun, when there's work to be done?" Gramps objected angrily. "Weeds are already o'ertaking the potatoes! Time and tide wait for no man!"

Grandma stepped up close to Gramps and tapped his chest. She had to reach up to do it. "I know some of your English sayings too, Frank," she said in her Swedish accent. " 'All work and no play makes Yack a dull boy.' I'm taking these two Yacks to the lake. Those older kids you hired can hoe the potatoes."

Grandma had saved a little each week from her regular creamery check, and now had enough to rent a cottage on the shore of Big Lake for a whole week. Mom was coming too. The boys were overjoyed.

Big Lake technically belonged to the Fond du Lac Reservation, but white vacationers and white business people from Cloquet and Duluth had bought up much of the shoreline. Brower's Resort was on the east side of the lake, only a few miles from Grandma's. There were cabins in a grove of pines, a dock for swimming, and boats they could use for fishing. All week, the boys swam with other kids and went fishing. Grandma and Mom mainly took it easy, but Grandma did some fishing too. She liked tiny sunfish, fried. Dad came on the weekend. It was a grand time.

After all that fun, it was hard to go back to the drudgery in Gramps' fields. The work seemed endless. As the vegetables ripened, the boys and hired laborers picked and prepared them for delivery. They had to be sorted, washed, trimmed, bundled and boxed. Peas, green corn, beans. Cucumbers, tomatoes, beets. Potatoes, onions, squash.

Cultivating potatoes could have been fun, if it hadn't been for Gramps' bad temper. Jim rode Morgan, seated on a gunny sack thrown over the horse's harness. He guided Morgan between the rows of potatoes, pulling a little cultivator. Gramps walked behind, holding the cultivator. Every so often Morgan stepped on a potato plant, squashing the potatoes near the surface, and Gramps yelled and swore and threw a clump of dirt at Morgan' hindquarters. Surprised, Morgan jumped, the gunny sack slipped, and Jim, also taken by surprise, had all he could do to hang on. In the process Morgan often trampled another half-dozen plants and Gramps swore even more, making Jim and Morgan so nervous they had a hard time driving straight for another row or two.

Riding those long rows, Jim had time to think about that. When one small thing went wrong, Gramps' anger made many more things go wrong; and that made him madder, which made even more things go wrong. Jim decided he wouldn't do that when he got big. *I might as well start learning how to control my temper right now,* he thought. He still felt mad at Gramps, though...

A week later, Gramps drove into the yard in a new blue pickup truck. He had bought it with the "fire money" that finally came through from the railroad. The Great Fire of 19 years earlier had been ignited by sparks from locomotives, and the railroad was finally settling with those who lost property. Gramps had lost a barn.

He let Bud and Jim climb in and look the truck all over. It smelled new; the chrome and dials were shiny. Gramps rigged it up as a delivery truck, and at first Jim was eager to go along to help.

But eventually, Gramps' sour temperament outweighed the fun of riding in the new truck. One day, after Jim and Bud loaded vegetables, Gramps pointed at Jim and then at the pickup.

"You're coming with me," he said.

"Awww..." He had been looking forward to playing with Bud while Gramps was in town. Bud had a fan from an old car and already had figured out how to fly with it: He was going to run along the roof of the barn and take off from there. Jim sure didn't want to miss that.

"'Awww' nothing," Gramps said. "Get in the truck."

Gramps was silent as they drove toward Cloquet's boarding houses, where loggers, sawmill workers and railroad men rented rooms. The renters ate together, family-style, in the main dining room, and Gramps kept the boarding house cooks supplied with vegetables. The first stop was Dube's Saloon and Boarding House, where the cook, Mrs. Sullivan, gave Jim a cheery greeting in her Irish brogue. Then to the Toivola Boarding House. The tall Finnish cook there never said anything. She looked hot and tired as she stirred gravy with one hand and checked a cauldron of boiling potatoes with the other. Jim felt sorry for her. The next stops were the Northeastern Hotel and the Anchor Inn on Dunlap Island.

Gramps pulled up to the Inn with an expectant, almost cheerful attitude. "Unload that stuff and then get back in the truck and wait for me," he said, and went inside.

Jim took boxes of vegetables around the back and into the kitchen. He was curious. Grandma had told him not to go into the place; there was a lot of drunkenness there, and fighting too. Gramps said that Stella, who was one of the owners, was even a better cook than Grandma. Jim meandered to the next room and peeked around a corner into a dining room. He didn't see any drunks, but he saw a lot of men sitting at a big table, eating roast beef and mashed potatoes. Gramps was eating there too. The sight made Jim so hungry he could hear his stomach growl. Gramps didn't see him, and Jim returned to the truck.

Almost an hour later, Gramps came back, weaving slightly. He was picking his teeth with a toothpick, and smelled like beer and smoke. He tossed Jim a Baby Ruth candy bar. *Yeah, you get a roast beef dinner and I get this*, Jim thought sourly. Then he remembered he wasn't going to be mad at anything, and he asked the Lord to take the sourness away. It worked, a little.

Their next deliveries were to private homes. Gramps parked along residential streets and honked the horn. Women came out and chose their vegetables, and some left orders for the next delivery. Jim carried their purchases into their kitchens. Many of the kitchens were fancy, with the latest electric refrigerators, and shiny counters bearing pop-up toasters and tabletop radios. In the small communities outside of Cloquet, the kitchens were plainer. Where customers were poor, Gramps charged half price.

Finally, there were only three bags of potatoes and a bunch of onions left. Gramps pulled up to a cabin on the south shore of Big Lake.

"Take that stuff in there, and don't charge her anything," he said.

Inside the cabin, Jim ducked a blanket hammock hanging from the ceiling; a thin Indian baby was in it. He also noticed two washtubs holding dirty water, and two skinned rabbits on the table. A tired-looking woman nodded her thanks as he set the packages on the floor by the wood stove.

Jim went back to the truck, and Gramps pulled out onto the road and turned toward home.

"Your grandmother is always saying that the Lord helps those who help themselves," he growled. "But that Indian woman is a widow - her husband got killed on the railroad a few months ago. She's doing all she can, and where's that Lord of yours, eh?"

Jim didn't know the answer. But he wasn't going to let grumpy Gramps fill his heart with doubt and spoil his faith. There had to be a good answer.

Grandma was pickling young beets when he entered the summer kitchen.

"Gramps said the Lord doesn't really help people who help themselves," he said. "He said some people try hard and God doesn't even care."

If Grandma had been a horse, her ears would have pricked straight up. Her back went straight and rigid and she turned to face him. She pointed a long spoon that was red with beet juice. "No man understands the Lord's design, boy, and don't you forget it. It's not for us to judge. Our job is to do our best as Christians and leave the rest in the Lord's hands."

"But what if He lets little children starve?"

"Then our job is to help those children - with prayer for sure, and with food if we can. We are not to judge the ways of Almighty God."

Jim tossed a beet into his mouth and went back outdoors. Chewing, half conscious of the explosion of smoky-sweet flavors, he thought about that answer. It didn't exactly satisfy him, although he was glad that Gramps had been doing God's job. He paused in the yard, swallowed the beet, and said a prayer for the Indian lady, her baby, and the tall tired Finnish cook. But he still didn't see why God wouldn't just point His finger and *ping!* make their troubles disappear.

Then he thought of another question and returned to the kitchen.

"How come a lot of Indian houses are poor and kind of dirty?"

Grandma turned to him again. "A lot of white houses are poor and dirty too. What about the Murphys, or the Larsons? Sometimes people are just down on their luck. We don't judge them. Never. Don't judge the ways of the Lord, and don't judge His children, either."

He liked that answer better. He went out to find Bud to see if he had been able to fly.

*   *   *

Mom felt tired and weak all through the winter and well into the following summer. Grandma took her to see Dr. Alfred Peterson, a Christian man and a homeopathic chiropractor. Dr. Peterson prescribed fresh fruit and long rests outdoors, preferably among balsam trees where Elizabeth could breathe in their healing fragrance.

Jim knew just the place back in the woods - a growth of tall balsams where the ground was free from underbrush and padded with dry balsam needles. In the summer heat, the air was sweet with balsam perfume. He strung up a hammock between two of the trees, and Elizabeth, with a grateful sigh, settled into it.

"This is perfect, son," she said. "So comfortable. Thank you."

Now for the fruit, Jim thought. There were canned peaches and canned plums in the house, but Dr. Peterson had specified fresh fruit in season. Jim checked the neighbor's apple tree; the apples hanging there were still green. So were the wild plums and chokecherries. The raspberries were already done for the year. He paused near the raspberry brambles. Something about the smell of things, the feel of the air and the angle of the sun was reminding him.... oh sure! Last year at this time he and Bud picked blueberries.

He trudged around a swampy area to the drier open meadow where they had picked last year. And there were the low bushes, looking blue with fat berries. He could see several people picking in the distance, across the meadow. He scooped a handful off a tiny branch and funneled them into his mouth; they were full-flavored, sweet and juicy. A few Juneberry trees edged the patch, and he nibbled on those sweet mealy berries too. He went home to fetch a small pail, and picked it full.

Mom ate some straight from the pail as she lay on the swaying hammock, and later in the house had a big dishful of berries and filabunk.

During the following week he and Bud had to pick green sweet corn for Gramps, but each evening they went to the blueberry patch. They picked enough to sell, and with his share of the money, Jim bought a World bicycle.

As a bonus, Mom was feeling better, and her improvement seemed to give Dad a lift. Amazingly, he asked the boys if they wanted to join the Scouts. A troop was starting in Knife Falls Township, and Dad would supply the land for a meeting shack, on a knoll at the edge of their 15 acres.

Dad, doing something for his boys? That made Jim even happier than being a Scout. But scouting was fun too. Their leader, Norm Poupore, loved to laugh and always thought up interesting projects and activities - camping, hiking, building.

That winter, though, scouting activities were smothered by snow. It fell and fell and kept on falling; too deep for them to use the shack; too deep even to meet anywhere. Jim was snowed in at Grandma's for a whole week, and he and Bud had to tunnel walkways from the house to the garage and barn. In their spare time they pumped buckets of water and poured them on the hills of snow, creating icy runs for fast, gasping rides on their sleds. Gramps plowed the driveway with a V-sled plow and the team of horses - primarily, it seemed, so that he could go out drinking.

One late evening they were all up waiting for him. Bud saw his lights swing in toward the garage. The lights went off, the plume from the exhaust disappeared - Gramps had turned off the car. But he didn't come in.

Ten minutes passed. Bud rubbed away the frost from the window so he could see the thermometer hanging outside. It was already 8 below. "We better go get him," Bud said.

"Naah, you leave him right there," Grandma snapped. "That big drunken lunkhead can sit there and freeze for all I care!"

Bud silently pulled on his overshoes and buckled them with slow deliberation. His face was set. "Come on, Jim, I'm going to need help."

Grandma's eyes snapped, and she turned to Jim. "You leave him be!" she ordered.

But he could see she was acting tougher than she felt. She was just mad at Gramps; she didn't really want him to freeze. He put on his coat and followed Bud.

Gramps was unconscious and too heavy for them. Bud got a sled and they pulled Gramps down from the seat and onto the sled as gently as they could. It slid to the entryway easily enough, but it took them awhile to pull it up the step and into the house.

Grandma stood by the doorway, her lips tightly pursed and her hands on her hips. Jim thought she was going to block the door, but Bud calmly kept going as though she weren't there, and she reluctantly made way for him.

"Put the sled over by the stove," she sighed. "He can sleep it off where he lays."

As Gramps warmed up, he started snoring, and the smell of beer filled the kitchen. Grandma blew out the lantern and the three went to bed. Later Grandma went back and covered Gramps with a quilt.

Spring came, and Dad's mood remained good. He wasn't drinking as much as before, and the low-toned late discussions about Dad chasing women ceased. Dad even got active with the Men's Brotherhood of Bethany Covenant Church in Cloquet.

He decided to surprise Mom with a greenhouse, something she had wanted for years. Jim helped him build it; Dad called it a Chinese style building. Mom was so pleased tears came into her eyes. She soon had seedlings started, flowers and vegetables, and by fall she also had ornamentals that she brought indoors. Several were poinsettias, and by December they were brilliantly red.

Jim had been looking forward to having some fun during Christmas break, until he learned he and Bud would have to spend it cutting wood with Gramps.

The ground was frozen hard and covered with snow, and perfect for logging. Bud and Jim hitched Morgan and Florry to the sleigh while Gramps sharpened the axes. It was 5 below, and the horses' breath made clouds around them. They warmed the bits under their armpits, inside their jackets, before sliding them into the horses' mouths.

Gramps' wood lot, a stand of popple, wasn't very far from the house. When they arrived, they tossed blankets over the horses and built a fire. It looked and felt cheerful there in the cold. Gramps' double-bitted axe cut easily into the soft popple wood. He felled trees as the boys trimmed off the branches and piled the slash to one side. Jim remembered hearing that timber slash like this had contributed to the Great Fire, but there was no point in mentioning it to Gramps. They soon got hot and removed their jackets.

At noon, Grandma appeared through the woods, a small rosy-cheeked figure against the white snow and gray-brown trees. She was carrying a Karo syrup bucket full of steaming coffee and a bag of sandwiches. After they ate by the fire, Gramps went back to cutting and the boys hauled sleigh loads of the 20-foot poles to Gramps' yard. The sleigh runners whispered through the snow, and the horses' straining bodies gave out a rich warm aroma that blew briefly into their faces before evaporating into the icy air.

Every day for a week, Gramps felled trees and the boys trimmed and hauled them home. By the end of vacation, Gramps' yard was piled high with wood. Next summer he would bring in a saw rig, and they would cut it up and stack it. This year's warm house was a result of last year's harvest.

*   *   *

Despite the hardships of the little log chapel, the congregation was growing. Grandma, Elizabeth and the Dorcas Ladies Aid society decided to look for a bigger building.

The Perch Lake Town Hall along Big Lake Road was no longer in use. Grandma's neighbor, Martin Kotiranta, was a Carlton County commissioner, and she asked him whether they could buy it.

"Now what would you ladies want with an old tin building that has holes in the roof?" he asked.

Grandma told him, and a week later he let her know: The congregation could buy the old town hall for a small fee. They found the money, patched the leaks, and the Tin Church, as it was called, became their place of worship. Still heated with wood, still lit with lanterns, it was nevertheless a real building and roomy besides, and they owned it. It was several years before the parishioners had completely remodeled the place, installed an oil furnace and electricity, and transformed the Tin Church into Big Lake Chapel.

That autumn of 1940 was unusually warm. Well into the second week of November, lazy flies continued to swarm in the sunshine, and people went outdoors in shirtsleeves. On Monday, the temperature reached a balmy 60. Then suddenly, the wind turned, and in a matter of minutes the temperature plummeted 25 degrees. Clouds blew in; rain started falling; a fierce wind picked up. The rain turned to snow, the temperature dropped to 15, and the wind became a gale. Gramps herded his cows into the barn and stabled Morgan and Florry. When he finished, the wind-driven snow was so thick he could hardly see his way back to the house. In another 20 minutes the mercury dipped below zero.

Later they heard on the radio that Cloquet had been on the edge of a freak storm that swept through the Midwest. Forty-nine Minnesotans, mostly stranded duck hunters, perished. In addition, 40 people in nearby states and 59 sailors on the Great Lakes died.

Blizzards continued through the winter, and the snow grew deeper and deeper. Six weeks after Jim's 13th birthday, another massive snowstorm hit, and 31 people perished.

Meanwhile, Northwest Paper laid off Dad, and money was tighter than ever. Dad's mood soured, and he gradually went back to his old habits. Jim often had to go in search of him. Sometimes he found Dad's car parked behind some moonshiner's house, or behind the house of a lady friend. Sometimes he could convince his drunken father to come home.

One late afternoon, after he had located but been unable to retrieve his father, Jim bicycled home to find a strange car in the yard. Inside, seated with Mom at the kitchen table, was an old lady. Mom motioned him over to the table, which was loaded with pack-ages - eggs, meat. He sat down and looked from the packages to the visitor.

"Do you remember who this is, Jim?" she asked.

The old woman smiled at him and reached out a hand to his cheek. She had sky-blue slanted eyes, and her hand was skinny and had big blue veins and brown spots. She looked pleasant enough, but he was getting a little tired of women always mothering him, and he definitely didn't like being petted by a stranger. "I don't think so," he said as coldly as he could without Mom noticing.

"This is Dad's mother - your Grandma Lydia."

Oh, yeah, now he remembered. He had met her before she divorced Grandpa John Esala. She had moved up north somewhere with her new husband. He smiled and said hello.

She beamed at him. "You good big my *poika*," she said, and then added a long sentence he couldn't understand. He recognized the Finnish word for "boy," so he figured the rest must be Finnish too.

"Grandma Lydia doesn't know much English," Mom explained.

"What did she say?"

Mom laughed. "Do you think I understand Finnish?"

Grandma Lydia waited for Dad until dark. To Jim's relief, he didn't show up; Grandma Lydia finally gave up and left. After she drove away, Mom started giggling.

"We were having coffee and coffeecake here, and trying to have a conversation," she said. "And Grandma Lydia was telling me about how tired she was, because she had been taking care of somebody's babies all summer." Mom paused. "At least, that's what I thought she was saying. She made a sound of a baby crying, and rocked her arms like a baby was in them. Then she counted in English, to show how many she was caring for." Mom started laughing hard. "'Wan, doo, tri, four, fie, six, sen, eight, nine, ten, leven'… the number kept going up, and I must have looked shocked, because she stopped counting and made the baby sound again, and then I realized…." Mom could hardly talk, she was laughing so hard. "She was baa-ing! They were sheep! She was telling me how many lambs had been born on their farm this spring!"

Mom sighed and fell to thinking. "Did you find him?" she finally asked.

He nodded.

"Where?"

Jim hated to say it. Dad was with a lady, and they were both drunk. Dad was so drunk he couldn't even walk.

Mom held up her hand. "Never mind, Jim. I don't even want to know."

The meat Grandma Lydia gave them was lamb. Mom brought a leg of lamb over to Grandma's, and she fixed it the way Gramps wanted it - roasted, with mint sauce. Jim thought it was delicious.

*   *   *

A Sunday school was initiated that fall in the Big Lake Chapel. On a Sunday in early October, two new girls came. Jim regarded them curiously. The hems of their dresses were wet, but the rest of their clothing, even their shoes and long stockings, was dry. He tried to figure out how that could have happened. He must have been staring at their legs, because Bud poked him; the teacher was casting him a warning look.

After Sunday school, he saw the girls standing shyly off to one side. He had to satisfy his curiosity. He went over and told them his name.

They introduced themselves: Mamie and Saimi Kiihiala. "Is Mr. Esala your father?" Saimi asked.

Well of course, Jim thought. *That was a dumb question.* "Do you know my dad?"

"Oh sure, we live just on the other side of his place."

Jim was confused. "His" place? Why not "your" place?

Then Mamie spoke up. "Do you live with your mother?" Saimi nudged her sister, scowling a little, and Mamie got flustered. "Oh, I'm sorry...I only - I wasn't - " She gave up, blushing, and looked at the ground, staring at the fallen popple leaves shining golden in the sun.

An awkward silence ensued. Suddenly it came together in Jim's mind - the Esala who was living alone, the wet dresses. "Do you live near Twin Lakes Road?"

They nodded.

Grandpa John Esala lived along a dip in the road that frequently was flooded, apparently from some underground sinkhole. The county kept hauling in rock and gravel for fill, but it kept right on flooding. People said that once a horse had sunk out of sight there. He looked at the girls' clean, dry shoes.

"Was the road flooded today?"

61

They nodded. "It was pretty high," Saimi said. Noticing Jim's interest in their shoes, she added, "We took them off to go through."

Jim was impressed. These October nights were close to freezing; that water must have been bone-numbing cold. The sisters sure wanted to get to Sunday school. He explained that their neighbor was his grandfather. "We live over by Swanson Road," he added.

The girls rarely missed Sunday school. They trudged through heavy snow and spring rains, and the hems of their dresses were often wet. Their father thought church was bunk, and refused to take them.

Not long after that, they got word that Grandpa John Esala was very sick. Jim, Bud and their parents went to visit him. Dad's sister Lempi made them coffee. Grandpa John looked old and tired; Dad hardly talked to him. Later, on the way home, Mom suggested that maybe they should bring Grandpa John to their house and take care of him. Dad said no.

"But Walfred, he's your father."

"He never acted like one."

"Does it matter? 'Honor thy father and thy' -"

Dad smacked the steering wheel. "Don't preach at me! That old man threw me out a long time ago, and did he ever help me or my family since? Not once! My mother couldn't even live with him!"

Mom was silent.

"I don't owe him a thing," Dad continued. "Anyway, Lempi's not married, she can take care of him. Don't ever bring it up again."

Mom didn't. But when Grandpa John died not long after the new church was built, Mom made sure he had a funeral there. It was the Big Lake Chapel's first funeral.

*   *   *

Jim was milking their cow on an unseasonably warm December evening when Bud made a surprise visit.

"We got bombed."

Bombed? Jim hadn't heard any booming sounds. The explosion must have happened downwind and miles away. He stood up, carefully swinging the bucket out from under Margaret, and nudged the stool to one side with his foot.

"Where? Is anybody hurt?"

"Over in Hawaii - hundreds of sailors are dead... It was Japan who did it. They bombed American ships over there. Surprise attack."

In the house, Dad and Mom, wearing absorbed, shocked expressions, were listening to the radio. The Japanese were bombarding American bases in the Philippines too.

"We're at war, boys," Dad said.

The next day at school, everyone was talking about it - the dirty rotten sneak attack on Pearl Harbor, the declaration of war. It wasn't long before many of the older boys, eager to fight the Japs, were enlisting.

"Man, I wish I could go," Bud announced at the following Sunday's dinner. Gramps looked up from his boiled dinner.

"Likely you'll get the chance," he said. "The last time those Jerries decided to rule the world, it took us four years to put them in their place."

"Not 'Jerries,' Gramps. 'Japs.'"

"I'm talking about the bloody Germans. Some of those friends of yours will be sent to Europe, to fight that blighter Hitler. We're in his war now too, you know."

Change came fast with America in the war. Gas, tires and food were rationed. Flags went up everywhere. Patriotic slogans appeared on walls, posters, calendars. Jobs opened up.

Dad landed a job in construction with the government, but he'd have to go far away to work it.

"How far?" Mom asked.

"Pretty far."

Mom's voice got stern. "Where, Walfred?"

Dad looked away. "Greenland."

"Greenland!" Mom exclaimed, her eyes wide. "The Greenland over by Sweden?"

"Well, it's not really by Sweden…"

"Greenland! Walfred!"

"The money's good, Elizabeth - $3 an hour, and room and board too. I haven't got a choice."

Dad left in March. He sent color postcards from Greenland. It didn't look green.

*   *   *

After dinner at Grandma's one Sunday, Bud left the table early. Jim found him upstairs, packing a suitcase.

"What's that?" Jim asked.

"My stuff."

"Yeah, well?"

"I'm moving to your - back to the - back home. Grandma said it's okay."

Jim watched in stunned happiness as Bud casually closed his suitcase and started down the stairs.

"Do you want to?"

"Yep."

And that was that. Bud was home again. Jim felt like he had a continually renewing Christmas present: his brother, every day.

They decided to raise chickens. Bud was handy with tools, and they rebuilt the Scout shack. They padded it with straw and hung warming lights overhead. Then they drove to the feed mill in Carlton and bought 100 chicks. The chicks looked like little yellow balls tumbling every which way under the light. On warm days, they let them out to scratch in the new grass of the yard.

On one such day, the brothers were returning from an errand at a neighbor's and noticed a black cloud rolling in from the west until it blotted out the afternoon sun. Suddenly the air turned icy cold, and rain started falling. The rain turned to hail.

"The chicks!" Bud yelled, and they ran home.

The yard was littered with little bodies. Not one chick was left standing. They brought several into the house to show Elizabeth.

"Quick, bring them all in," she said, as she opened the oven door of her electric range and set the thermostat on low.

They put trays full of chicks in the warm oven. Soon the limp little bodies were stirring, and it wasn't long before dozens of cheeping chicks were darting around the kitchen.

They grew fast. Between taking care of chicks and working in Gramps' fields, the brothers didn't have much free time that summer. When the chickens were big enough, the boys killed, plucked and gutted every one. The smell of wet chicken feathers and chicken guts was nauseating. Jim thought he'd never be able to eat chicken again. George Bryant at Bryant's Store bought all the chickens, and the boys used $50 to buy a 1928 Model A stock car. It had 21-inch wheels and was in mint condition

Bud used it to get to Duluth, where he had enrolled in a trade school. His "A" classification for gas rationing allowed him barely enough gas - four gallons a week - to get to his classes.

Jim caught a ride into Cloquet with him one day, and instead of going to school he hung around the YMCA and played pool. About the time school was letting out, he stopped playing pool and walked home. On the way, he noticed Blue Star Mother flags hanging in some windows. One window had two stars - two sons were in the war. In another window hung a Gold Star Mother flag, showing that the son had been killed.

He was mulling that over when he got home. Mom was at the table, reading a letter. She looked up at him.

"How was school?"

Jim squirmed inside. "Okay…got any buns?"

"In the breadbox." Mom held up the letter. "It's from your father. He's in Alaska."

Jim buttered two buns and sat across from her to eat them, and she began reading aloud:

I can't tell you where I am exactly, because of the war there are censors who check all the mail. I don't think there's a town anyplace around here anyhow for you to find on a map even if they had a map for this wilderness which they don't. We're building a Road through the roughest country I ever saw, if it's not steep mountains then it's muskeg so bad it makes northern Minnesota look like a dry desert, even though it's 50 below your feet can still go through the ice and get wet and then have you got trouble. We live in tents and just about freeze day and night. Lots of frozen cheeks and toes in our gang, one boy got hauled out to a hospital I am sure he will lose his foot. They got Colored troops working here too, almost 4000 of them, they are from hot weather country like Mississippi and they do pretty good for boys who never even saw 10 below let alone 79 below like it was last month. I guess I should not complain about the cold, I hear that in the summer the mosquitoes here are worse than anything we got at home not to mention grizzly bears. This is a big project, one of the engineers said it's bigger than the Panama Canal, and they have thousands of Soldiers working for Uncle Sam and then us Civilians working for Reese & Olson, or their subcontractors I should say. The Soldiers have got it worse than us some-times they work 20 hours a day and not as good food as we get. Over in the Aleutian Islands our boys are still fighting the Japs and that is not far enough away from us for my money but I guess we are safe here if the grizzlies don't get us. Your husband Walfred. P.S. Say Hi to the boys I sure will be glad to see Home again.

Jim tried to imagine 79 degrees below zero, and his father sleeping in a tent. He pictured Dad with wet freezing feet and numb fingers, and no place to get warm in…Dad was going through a lot on behalf of the family. The thought softened him toward his father.

"Let's pray for him together," Mom said after a long silence. Jim bowed his head too and tried to let the spirit of her prayer enter him. But his playing hooky made him feel like a liar and a hypocrite, and he had trouble staying focused.

He later learned that his father had been working on a 1,500-mile-long highway between Dawson Creek, near the British Columbia-Alberta border, and Fairbanks, Alaska. The job was completed in eight months and eventually became known as the Alcan Highway.

*   *   *

One of the brothers' friends, Paul Salmi, had a 1936 Ford. On a sparkling winter day the three boys took three girls for a ride. Ellen and Dorothy Vafias were sisters, and they had a girl cousin from Greece who was staying with them. Paul drove to the north end of Big Lake - and then straight down onto the frozen surface. The girls shrieked, especially the Greek who didn't understand how strong lake ice could be. The lake was smooth as glass

"There's not a pimple on it!" Jim observed in amazement. Usually the lake froze in bumps or broken sheets, and had a covering of snow as well.

Paul floored the gas pedal, and raced the car wide open across the lake. Suddenly the lakeshore on the south end looked awfully close. Paul shifted down; the Ford slid straight on. He braked; on they went. Rocks along the shore seemed to be flying toward them. The girls screamed; Jim braced himself. Paul turned the wheel hard and the car spun around and around. They slid to a soft, safe stop and sat in shocked silence for awhile. Then they all started laughing.

"Let's go again!" Jim yelled.

But the girls wanted to go home.

*   *   *

On Friday and Saturday nights, Bud liked to go to town and hang out with friends, and he let Jim tag along. Mom wasn't happy with what she called their "gallivanting," but she didn't try to stop them. Jim felt grown-up and only a little guilty when he bought his first pack of cigarettes. He liked store tobacco a lot better than the Indian tobacco he and Bud had smoked behind the Whippet garage on the farm when they were kids. And drinking beer or wine with Bud and his friends didn't seem so bad, either.

Once in awhile there was a fight; Jim found out he could hold his own.

He continued attending church, but it didn't seem as interesting as it had before. He knew Mom was feeling bad about his cooling faith; to make her feel better, he sometimes left his open Bible on his bed, so she would think he'd been reading it. It was surprising how quickly he got out of the habit of reading the Bible, though. He didn't even miss it. Maybe Mom and Grandma went a little overboard on that religion stuff.

*   *   *

Not long after Bud's 17th birthday, as the three Esalas were sitting at the dinner table, Bud announced that he was going to join the Navy. Mom didn't even glance up from her plate, but her hands became still. Jim stopped eating and stared at his brother. Bud had been saying right along that he was going to enlist, but somehow Jim didn't think it would really happen. He figured the war would end, or Bud would change his mind.

"You're too young," Mom said.

"Not if you sign for me."

"Why would I do that? I don't want you to go."

"But Mom, all the guys are signing up… Besides, it's our patriotic duty."

Mom's face got stubborn. "Your father's doing enough patriotic duty for this family right now."

Bud tried a different tack. "Well, if I don't enlist in the Navy, probably I'll get drafted into the Army pretty soon anyway. What would you rather have, me in the infantry in the jungle, with Japs shooting at me from everywhere and poison snakes crawling in my blankets, or safe on a ship?"

Mom was keeping track of the war; she knew the infantry casualty rates were dreadfully high, three times as high as the Navy's. But sailors were in the thick of it too and dying by the thousands on ships that were safe only if nobody bombed them. "That boat they sank over in Hawaii…"

"The *Arizona*," Bud interrupted. "It's a ship."

Bud rarely interrupted, but Mom didn't seem to notice.

"Sailors' bodies are still inside it. And the war's even worse now. I can't let my own boy become one of those bo -" The very thought of it elicited a sob, which she choked back. "- those bodies; I just can't."

But Bud kept pestering her, and two weeks later she relented. Once again Bud was moving away, and it seemed to Jim he had only just come home after so many years. A profound sadness descended on him as his brother's train pulled out. It was more than sadness; he felt broken, like his left arm was gone, and there was a terrible ache in his heart.

Bud went to Farragut, Idaho, for basic training, and then he disappeared into the vast Pacific, eventually writing from a faraway island called Kwajalein. Mom put up a Blue Star flag, and she prayed mightily that it never would change its color.

*   *   *

71

Jim got in the habit of skipping school and playing pool. A couple of other boys sometimes skipped with him. Some of the guys had girlfriends, and they spent their gas allotment for late-night drives down private back roads. Jigs Olson had lots of girls, and he would come back from his trysts swaggering and bragging about what he had done with the girls.

Jim was silent, disapproving. That was one thing he wasn't going to do until he met the right woman and got married.

"What's your problem, Esala, you afraid of the babes?" Jigs sneered. "Or maybe you're a sissy boy, huh?"

Jim had trained himself to disregard Gramps' needling, and he wasn't about to let Jigs, an amateur compared with Gramps, get to him. "I think you're the one that doesn't like girls, Jigs. If you did, you wouldn't treat them so bad."

"Hah! I give them all my love."

Jim felt disgusted. "That's not love, when you use people like that."

"People? Man, they're just girls! That's what they're for!"

Jim's stomach turned. Why was he hanging around this guy, anyhow? *I might not read the Bible anymore,* he thought, *but I'm still a believer.* And he believed that God meant for one man and one woman to love one another, for their whole lives.

Later, walking home, he thought about marriage. All that fighting - Mom and Dad, Gramps and Grandma. It seemed like they couldn't figure out how to be happy with one another. On the surface, it looked like Gramps and Dad were at fault, but he knew Grandma's personality had something to do with it. She was good-hearted, but she controlled everybody, especially Mom. *Look at how she took Bud away. Dad should have stood up to her.* Mom told him once that Dad stood up to Grandma on one occasion, and that was when Bud was a new baby. Grandma had decided to name him, and Dad had put his foot down.

He realized he was feeling a little mad at Grandma. He didn't like the feeling and put it to one side. It was easier being mad at Gramps.

When he got home that evening, he saw a thin, pale man sitting at the table drinking tea. The warm kitchen smelled like beer. Jim looked closer. The man was Dad.

"Hiya, Pootie," he slurred, and grinned a little crookedly.

Mom's mouth was set in a grim line. "Yah, your father's home again. Same as always."

Jim looked from his mother to his father and back again. He looked at the table, the sink, the kitchen walls.

I want to get out of here, he thought. *I want my own life.*

Shirley

*S*hirley's mother was spoiling her. Her mother loved babies, and she wanted to keep her last child a baby as long as possible. Little Shirley could do no wrong; her every wish was gratified. The little girl became especially close to her teenaged brother James, who became a second father to her.

The family was a little concerned about her language development. By age 4 she still had not said one word. But one day James and their father were working on a pump on the family farm, when their mother and Shirley approached. And Shirley said her first words, as plain as day: "Hey James! What are you doing there?" Apparently she had felt comfortable in her safe little baby cocoon, and just didn't feel like talking until then. She never stopped.

Although James' high school days were full with studies and with athletics, he gave a lot of attention to his little sister. He worried that the coddling their mother gave her was *ill preparing her for life. But then, when Shirley was 6, James went off to college, and the little girl lost her best bro.*

A man with a grain of faith in God never loses hope, because he ever believes in the ultimate triumph of Truth….My heart continually says, "Rock of Ages, cleft for me, let me hide myself in thee."

- Gandhi

CHAPTER 4

Visits

Go forward in time again. On this weekday, white-haired Jim is sitting over coffee in what he calls "McDonald Marketplace Church." It's the Golden Arches in Cloquet, and still too early for the dominating fragrance of Big Macs. It's only 8 in the morning, and people are buying McMuffins and pancakes and lots of coffee.

A short slim man is sitting with him, and as I pull a chair over to the table, Jim introduces him. Larry. Larry is a long-distance bicyclist. Not the kind in Spandex shorts and biking helmet, but a man who is something of a hermit, whose clothes are loose and a little tattered - and who is extraordinarily bright and interesting.

We talk about his adventures on the hand-built bike of his own design, which are many: fighting masses of crickets while camped in the cornfields of Iowa; pedaling 6,000 miles in 60 days, losing 60 pounds in the process; the deer and bear with whom he has shared starlit nights.

Once in a while Jim brings in a comment about God's love, or how the Lord works in mysterious ways, and Larry skillfully sidesteps them. He doesn't want to talk religion, and Jim doesn't push it.

Other McDonald's customers stop by the table to greet Jim. They are affectionate and respectful, and some address him as "brother." Others, not wanting to interrupt us, ask if he'll be there tomorrow.

A middle-aged fellow whose blue eyes are sharp with curiosity approaches. He's been sitting nearby and was paying attention to the fact that I was taking notes. Jim introduces us - the man's name is Tom - and he tells Tom that I'm writing a book about his life. Larry shrinks back into a corner. He's not comfortable around people in general, but he clearly doesn't trust this man.

Tom grins in a disrespectful way and slaps Jim on the back. "You know this guy's a holy man, right?"

I tip my head noncommittally

"You've got to watch out for him. He's got powerful friends. Like God."

"Mmmm-hmmm."

"We all have a lot of regard for Jim. He's gonna be famous when this book you guys are writing comes out. You too. People are gonna flock to buy it, just flock." His tone sounds as though he'll be surprised if a single person is interested in reading it.

Apparently unaware of the sarcasm in the man's voice, Jim smiles. "Well, we're not looking at that, Tom. My only hope is that it gets through to people, softens some hearts so the Lord can enter in."

"Oh sure, that's what we all want all right. A lot of money would be nice, too." He almost snickers as he walks away, giving a brief, dismissive wave without looking back.

Larry glowers at Tom's back. Then he too rises to leave. He pauses by the table and turns back to me.

"When my whole world is falling apart, I go to see Jim," he murmurs. "Lots of people do. Many people." He thinks a moment, and then gestures towards himself, taking in his general street-personish appearance. "Jim accepts me even though I'm different. He accepts everybody. Everybody." Then he leaves.

Jim takes our cups and leaves to gets refills. Now I have a view of Tom, who is back at his table talking to another man - apparently about Jim and me, because they both throw me a glance.

When Jim returns, I ask him whether he thought Tom had been sincere about the book and about Jim being a "holy man."

"Well, no; he was being sarcastic," Jim replies. "I used to have that problem too, when I was younger. I could cut someone down pretty quick with my tongue. But the Lord took care of that."

"It seemed like he was belittling you…"

"That doesn't bother me. If it did, it wouldn't bring him any closer to the Lord, and it would take me farther from Him."

"You don't feel mad?"

"Nah. I never get mad, except maybe at the Devil. I'm not judgmental, I try not to be suspicious of people's motives; it's not my business. The Lord takes care of everything. I just do my best, and trust in Him."

We finish our meals, and then I ask Jim if he'll show me around his old stomping grounds, the places where he grew up. "Why, sure!" he responds exuberantly. "Where do you want to start?"

We start with Larch Avenue, his first childhood home, a lovely slope with fresh westerly breezes flowing over it. Then we visit graves at the nearby wooded cemetery - his grandparents', his parents'.

We move on to the Julius Coffee place - his second childhood home, where Jim's mother planted Norway pines and thawed the chicks, where he milked Margaret, where his father threatened his mother. Now the trees are towering, and lovely paths wind among bird feeding stations and flower beds. Bud's daughter Colleen now owns the place.

Next door is brother Bud's house, and Jim introduces me to him and Jenny, his wife. He's tall, dark and handsome; the family resemblance is strong. She is short and sunny. Their spotlessly clean home is a picture of loving attention, with careful landscaping and cheerful interior design.

As we leave, Jim explains why he's glad that his brother and brother's family now have the old homestead. "Property doesn't interest me," he said. "The only thing I own is this old car. If I had kept the family home, I would have had to spend my time keeping the lawn trimmed and the house painted. My brother and his wife have that real pretty place, right next door, and they put a lot of effort into keeping it that way - the yard, the flowers, everything. How would it be if over here there was a place that needed painting, where the grass didn't get cut or the snow shoveled, and weeds choked out the flowers? I'd feel responsible to keep the place up. But I'm not interested in that.

"What interests me is people. I want to spend my time talking to them, fellowshipping with them, helping them. Not painting the trim and digging in the perennial garden."

We drive by Grandma's and Gramps' old farm, and Grandpa John Esala's homestead, and we swing by the old Tin Chapel, which became Big Lake Church. Jim points out where Long Johnson lived and died.

Then we head toward a church that Jim and his prayer partners built several decades ago, on a five-acre parcel he had retained from the old family property. Since being a preacher and also corporate head of the Cloquet church wasn't really in his line, the place eventually closed. On the way, he explains why he likes the "McDonald Marketplace Church" better.

"I was never called to be a preacher or to build buildings," he said. "I get excited about being in the marketplace - Hardees, Wal-Mart. Wherever people gather in their everyday lives."

He pulls up in front of the building. I gulp. I've been here before. The unpleasant memory floods back…

It is maple sugar season, 1974. My estranged husband has brought me, our two small children, and his mother out on a Sunday drive, ostensibly to see a horse-drawn maple syrup operation, followed by dinner out - an effort to rebuild our relationship. His mother and I are cheerfully hopeful, and we chatter about the passing scene as we head toward Cloquet. But we become puzzled when he rushes us through the sugar operation, skips the meal and drives out of town, down a wooded lane and into a churchyard.

The church is way back in the woods. There are a lot of cars parked there. It's late in the day, and getting cold.

"What….what is this?" his mother asks.

He turns off the car, removes the keys and opens the door. "We're going in here."

I am in the back seat with the children - a three-year-old and a nursing baby. It's going to be too cold in the car for them pretty soon, and it's a long walk back to Cloquet. Anger floods me as I realize he has trapped us. His mother's dismayed voice is touched with a similar anger as she asks him to take us back to town, where we can wait for him. He refuses.

So we trail after him into the church and into a pew toward the front. The service, if that's what it is, has been going on for awhile. I try to figure out just where we might be in the ceremony - has the sermon already happened? The offertory?

But it's hard to figure out, because there seems to be no form to the ritual. The slightly built man who seems to be the leader is strutting around yelling "Jee-zus! Jee-zus!" Suddenly a woman near us leaps to her feet and begins jabbering loudly in a language that is totally unrecognizable as a human language - it has no form other than a kind of auctioneer's cadence.

"She's speaking in tongues," my husband whispers.

I've heard about that. It's one of the nine "gifts of the spirit" that charismatic Christians talk about. These gifts are supposedly special. But this woman's children register no surprise at her action; one is playing on the floor with toy cars and doesn't interrupt his play with so much as a glance upward. They're obviously used to her putting on a show like this.

She stops talking, and right on cue, the man in front begins "interpreting" - another "gift of the spirit" - for our edification. Also a showman, he uses a fractured King James English - a "thou" where a "thee" ought to be, a "ye" for a "you," and a "hast" for a "hath."

Right. Like God, who speaks only King James English, is sending us Minnesotans a divine message in a language that nobody here has ever used, and nobody in England has used for hundreds of years, and He doesn't even know how to speak it properly?

I feel disgusted on top of feeling angry and used. I can't stand these liars, but I don't know how to get out of here. Then, relief! The baby is hungry and begins fussing. He needs to nurse. Taking his sister with me,

I walk toward the back of the church, toward a little room I saw on the way in. As I move up the aisle, I notice the faces of people in the congregation - many open, believing faces. Honest faces.

We retire to the small room, which is just off the aisle. This is much better. A little light filters into the room, and I find some crayons and a coloring book to keep my daughter occupied. The baby nurses and gradually falls asleep to the drone of church voices.

Suddenly a loud yell pierces the peace; the baby's eyes fly open and he begins to cry. The loud voice is shouting angrily about brimstone and damnation and where we're all about to go. My daughter leaps to her feet, looking outraged: The bad man scared the baby! Before I can stop her, she jumps out into the aisle, puts her little hands on her hips, glares down the long aisle at the speaker, and shrieks,

"BEEEEEEE QUIET!!!!"

Sitting here in front of the same church with Jim, 30 years later, I wonder again if I really want to do this book. Is it possible that this honorable man sitting next to me was involved in the hypocrisy that I saw here firsthand? I know that the showman my daughter yelled at was not Jim. That man was much smaller, with a heart-shaped face and a cynical set to his lips.

"When did you have this church?" I ask Jim.

"Let me see - during the 70s."

"Did you have revivals here too?"

"Oh you bet, we had some rousing revivals here. Visiting preachers would come, and the place filled right up."

I look at him. He is genuine. I can feel it in my bones. Like some of the parishioners here 30 years ago, he is trusting of people, and faithful to God, and sincere. I already know what he would say if I griped about that showman and his sidekick - the jabbering woman who was probably also the showman's wife. Jim would react the same as he did toward the cynic at McDonald's: patiently, kindly, without judgment, but also like a rock - without compromising himself.

So I don't say anything about having been at his church, and decide to go on with the project.

*Human beings have come to a point where they
no longer know why they exist. They don't use the
knowledge that the Spirit has put into every one of
them; they are not even aware of this, and so they
stumble along blindly on the road to nowhere -
a paved highway which they themselves bulldoze
and make smooth so that they can get faster to the
big, empty hole which they'll find at the end,
waiting to swallow them up.*

- John Fire Lame Deer

CHAPTER 5

The War

J im awoke in the dark. It was his 17th birthday
- February 15, 1945. He quietly slipped on his
jacket, pulled on his boots and stepped outside into
the darkness. It wasn't very cold - maybe 10 above.
Those 30-below days of January were behind them
now. The sun wouldn't be up for another hour, but he
was too restless to wait. He walked in the direction

of town, enjoying the soft snowflakes falling on his face. His destination was the Post Office.

The sign on the door told him the office would open at 8. He peered through a window. The dim light of dawn showed the large face of a Seth Adams clock. It said 6:45. He paced back and forth to keep warm, stopping every so often to read the poster in the window: "Join the Navy and See the World." That was exactly what he intended to do.

*   *   *

Elizabeth was spooning thin Swedish pancake batter into a frying pan when Jim returned home.

"Mom."

Something in his voice made her look up, and some batter dribbled down the outside of the pan. She set down the bowl, a questioning and slightly alarmed look in her eyes.

Jim took a deep breath, and blurted it out: "I want to join the Navy."

Her hand went to her throat. "No!"

"Mom, I really want to help Bud. I've gotta go."

"No!" she repeated loudly. "I can't have both my boys over there in that awful place!"

Grandma was visiting; she came in from the other room, tying on an apron. "What's all this?" she demanded.

"Jim says he wants to join the Navy."

Jim turned to his grandmother. "I tried to enlist this morning, but they won't let me. I need Mom's signature."

"Well, she won't give it to you," Grandma said firmly. "You're not going to that Navy. That's all there is to it."

Elizabeth looked at Jim and nodded. That was all there was to it.

Jim found his father out by the shed, trying to start the car.

"Grandma and Mom are mad at me," he said. They were usually mad at Dad, and Jim figured his father would be more amenable to his request if he realized that Jim was on his side now - another man suffering the control of unreasonable women. It worked.

*   *   *

Meanwhile, the tide of war in the Philippines was beginning to turn. During that very week, General Douglas MacArthur, the supreme commander of allied sea, air and land forces in the Pacific, had fulfilled his pledge to return to the island chain. It had been almost three years since the Japanese had captured Manila and the Bataan Peninsula; MacArthur and American forces had been forced to leave the Philippines in March of 1942. The general's return was initiated the previous fall, when Vice Admiral Thomas Kinkaid's Seventh Fleet, Admiral William Halsey's Third Fleet and Lt. Gen. Walter Krueger's Sixth Army attacked Japanese entrenchments in the Philippines' Leyte Gulf and on the island of Leyte. There they encountered the first of more than 2,000 Japanese suicide bombers who would fly during the rest of the war - the kamikazes, which Halsey later said were the only weapons he feared.

Leyte secured, the Americans and allies struggled on through the long island chain. A day after Jim's 17th birthday, the U.S. 38th Infantry recaptured the Bataan Peninsula, the scene of such vast suffering, where an estimated 10,000 Americans and Filipinos died in April, 1942 on the infamous Bataan Death March. Two days after Jim's birthday, the 503rd Parachute Regimental Combat Team reclaimed the strategically placed guard island of Corregidor.

Jim and his dad went downtown to the Post Office, and Jim enlisted under his father's signature. Steeling himself against his mother's tears and his grandmother's protests, he bid them goodbye and headed for Duluth. The train there took him to the Great Lakes Naval Training Center on Lake Michigan. It was the first time he had been more than 30 miles from home.

While Jim was in training - being schooled as a motor machinist, jumping hurdles, being vaccinated, cleaning latrines - U.S. and Filipino troops re-took Manila. Although Japan was weakening, the situation was still critical: Japan had vowed to fight to the death; American forces remained divided between the Pacific and the war in Europe; and President Franklin D. Roosevelt had just died. Jim's group was hurried through boot camp in eight, instead of 16 weeks, herded into a troop train and shipped to San Francisco. At the Naval Training Center on Treasure Island, they were given rushed instruction in mustard gas protection, fire drills, swimming under fire and how to identify enemy planes. They went to Point Montara Anti-Aircraft Training Center, 25 miles from San Francisco, and learned how to operate ship weaponry - five-inch guns, 40-millimeter anti-aircraft guns with tracer bullets.

In the midst of anti-aircraft training one day in early May, an officer got on a megaphone and called for their attention. All guns stopped. All faces turned toward him.

"I have an announcement," he shouted, unable to keep the joy out of his voice. "President Truman has announced that the Germans have surrendered unconditionally."

The long war in Europe was over! The boys shouted, hooted, jumped - and fired. Whoever had a weapon, shot it. Jim was the breech man on a 5-inch gun; he grabbed a projectile off the stand, slid the shell into the gun, closed the breech block and let it rip. Everyone seemed to be shooting; the noise was deafening. For fifteen minutes, the rapid fire continued. The earth shook. Dirt and dust rose 18 inches from the ground. Empty wooden bullet boxes dropped away, fresh boxes were opened. The excitement was sensational.

As if some cosmic force demanded balance, the noisy, extreme excitement of that day was followed by silent, extreme boredom. The newly trained men were immediately sent back to Treasure Island - to wait. The end of the war in Europe had freed up forces for the Pacific, and the critical need for new men had suddenly evaporated. This overflow occurred during the highest Navy population of the war, tabulated that very week - 3.4 million people, with 68,000 vessels in the water.

Ready to go, all packed and trained and seaworthy, Jim's now redundant group sat on their sea bags in a fenced pen on the "grinder," the tarred parade ground. All day the hot sun beat on them, and they waited. In the evening, they unpacked; in the morning they packed in readiness again.

After three days of this, Jim had enough.

"Chief!" he called to his chief petty officer.

The short, stocky man came over to the fence. "What do you want, Esala?" he asked.

"I gotta get out of here. I can't wait until whatever ship we're scheduled for shows up here. Just ship me out on the next vessel, PLEASE?"

The CPO chuckled. "You'll wish you weren't so impatient when you get to where you're going," he said.

"Where's that?"

"Can't tell you. But just watch the board. Your orders will be up there in a few days."

Four more days passed, four days of heat and sun, of ready duffels, ready bodies, and utter boredom. Then the orders went up. The boys would ship out on the *USS Saratoga.*

The *Saratoga* was an aircraft carrier that had been hit by five kamikaze pilots at Iwo Jima just a few months earlier. She had limped into Puget Sound at Seattle for repairs, and on May 22, having been converted to a troop ship, she had left the Sound to pick up Jim's group in San Francisco. They were headed for Pearl Harbor in Hawaii.

The steep gangplank stretched out in front of Jim like a path to mystery, to his future, to a world of excitement. As he stepped onto it, a thrill went through him. Out to sea at last! What a trip this would be! And what a ship! The *Saratoga* weighed 33,000 tons and was 888 feet long. The flight deck was 75 feet above the keel; she could carry 80 planes and travel 34 knots. And she was underway.

They glided past Alcatraz Island and the federal prison there. Then under the Golden Gate Bridge. No sooner were they out to sea than several green-faced boys raced to the rail and threw up. Jim mentally checked his own stomach. He was proud and a little surprised to find it all shipshape. He had good sea legs, and never would experience nausea at sea.

He leaned on the rail, watching the waves and the beauty of the setting sun, into which they were sailing. Jim was no longer in the habit of praying, but the sight of this splendor brought a reflective peace to his spirit. *What an awesome God, who made all this*, he thought.

The next day, Jim saw a *Saratoga* crewman tying a new pair of work denims to a long line.

"What are you doing?" he asked.

"Gonna fade these out." The seaman attached the free end of the rope to the rail and threw the denims overboard. They bumped along the top of the water for awhile, and then, waterlogged, dragged on the line like a huge wiggling fish, barely visible under the surface. *So that's how these guys get to look like old salts*, Jim thought. His group had just been issued new work denims, and the boys looked like greenhorns in the bright blue jeans and stiff blue shirts. Jim found a rope and tossed his denims overboard too. Soon there were many ropes dragging from the ship. In the plunging sea water, the clothes softened and faded quickly.

As Jim stared down at the tugging lines, he wondered if Bud had done the same with his denims. Where was his brother now? Still at Kwajalein? Was that nearby? Jim studied the horizon. Maybe they were passing Bud's island right now. Flying fish sailed through the air, but he could see no island anywhere. The ship moved on over the smooth, calm surface of the ocean. The Pacific sure was big.

After four days out, moving an average of 28 knots, the *Saratoga* pulled into Pearl Harbor. Jim again stood at the rail, eagerly taking in the mountains, the palm trees, the ships in the harbor.

"Get a load of that ship," the next man on the rail said, lifting his chin toward a nearby battleship. "Looks new, don't she?"

Jim looked; the name on the side was the *Missouri*. Actually, she was not quite new: Launched the previous January, she had had been hit by a kamikaze at Iwo Jima not two months after the *Saratoga* was hit near the same island. A few months hence, the *Missouri* would be the site of the formal surrender of Japan.

The *Saratoga* docked, and a landing craft pulled up alongside. At first Jim's heart jumped, with the impossible hope that Bud, who had pulled Landing Craft Infantry duty, might be aboard. Of course, he wasn't. He was far away, maybe wounded, maybe dead.

All their sea bags had been piled on the deck, and the *Saratoga*'s crew started tossing the bags down into the LCI vessel. Jim and one of the other new seamen, Frenchy, stood together on the dock, watching the operation. It was a long way from the deck to the smaller craft below.

"One of those bags is going to miss, you just watch," Frenchy said.

The harbor water was filthy, with all those ships docking and pumping. Unrecognizable but definitely revolting things were floating in it. Sure enough, a couple of bags missed the landing craft, plunged into the dirty water, and bobbed there like large sponges. Jim and Frenchy laughed delightedly: The sorry owners of those filthy bags were in for a surprise! But later, when they came for their gear, Jim's humor evaporated. His was one of the soaked bags. Frenchy thought that was even funnier, and teased Jim as they hauled their bags through the gathering dark to their new quarters. Jim unpacked his gear and hung everything to dry. There was no place to do laundry.

There was no hurry, either. The seamen had arrived only to wait again, in another fenced-in bullpen, while high-level officers somewhere far away discussed who should go where, and by what means, and when, and for what task. This bullpen's only advantage over Treasure Island's was that Hawaii was cooler and sea breezes constantly flowed over them. But the wait was longer, and there was no leave for explorations of Honolulu. A few restless boys cut holes in the fence and went AWOL to see the sights, take in a movie, find a girl or get drunk, but Jim decided against accompanying them. The only views he ever got of Hawaii were from the ship and through the fence.

They waited a month. Finally, toward the end of June, they boarded a ship that seemed odd and small after the *Saratoga*. The *Letitia* was a 538-foot British hospital ship. She was fresh from the Atlantic and the war in Europe, where she first sailed as an armed merchant cruiser and troop ship, and later as a Canadian hospital ship. Now that Germany had surrendered, she was making her first trip into the Pacific to aid the war effort there.

The mostly Scottish crew was not happy with the Yanks. For one thing, there would be no more drinking with the Americans aboard. Alcohol was (and continues to be) allowed on British ships, but the *Letitia* now was sailing under U.S. Navy rules, and the Navy has prohibited alcohol since 1917. For another, the Scots had already fought their war, and here these Americans were dragging them across the globe to fight theirs. For a third, the Yanks would have no duty while aboard, and the Scots would do all the work. The Scots had reason to be resentful, and as the Americans boarded, the Scots glared at them.

The *Letitia* sailed southwest, at about half the speed of the *Saratoga*. The ocean was calm. Every day the heat and humidity grew more stifling. Jim developed a skin fungus, commonly called jungle rot. One of the four female nurses aboard told Jim he should expose his skin to the sunlight. *What,* Jim thought, *ALL my skin, with these women aboard? Not a chance.* But he would treat his upper body.

One day when the sun was out, he noticed an empty hammock swinging on the deck. It looked inviting. The Scottish crew was working, so the owner wouldn't need it. Jim slid into it, stretched out, raised his arms so the sun could hit his jungle-rot armpits, and looked into the blue sky above. The gentle rise and fall of the ship rocked the hammock slightly. He sighed in satisfaction and closed his eyes.

Suddenly somebody shouted; his eyes shot open; he saw a man rushing at him with a knife raised to strike. Jim rolled out and scrambled away on all fours, just as a Scot tumbled over the hammock from the other side, knife still in hand. The Scot's buddies grabbed him, took away the knife, and settled him down. Jim felt hot anger flood him, and he willed it into cool submission. The Scot plunked himself into his hammock and shot murderous looks at Jim.

"That guy sure must love his hammock," Jim said.

*   *   *

Several weeks and more than 5,000 miles later, the *Letitia* was nearing her destination. Jim leaned on the rail, straining to see the horizon. Dim outlines of volcanoes rose out of the rainy mist. What was ahead?

Their destination, it turned out, was Luzon, the main island in the Philippines, and Jim got his first sight of the destruction of war. Masts of sunken Japanese ships stuck out of Manila Bay. Up ahead, past Corregidor Island and the Bataan Peninsula, was what was left of a once lovely old city. Gone were Manila's 17th-century Spanish colonial homes and rich tropical vegetation. The city had been captured after weeks of hard fighting, which included artillery barrage from the advancing Americans and destruction of strategic buildings by the retreating Japanese. Most homes, businesses, ancient stone fortresses, other buildings and trees were now rubble and ruin. Nor were there many people around that Jim could see. Throughout the Philippines during the previous few months, almost one million Filipinos had died. At the same time, 140,000 Americans and 300,000 Japanese had been wounded or killed.

The ship anchored, and the wide-eyed, stiff-legged sailors disembarked in the rain, hauling their gear behind them. Jim felt disoriented but curious - curious about a tropical island, about devastated Manila, and about where they were going next.

A Filipino boy came toward them, dragging a cart. "American sailor! You like?" he called, and held up an empty cone and an ice cream scoop. An ice cream vendor! Where had he found ice in this hot place of destruction? The sailors queued up and bought cones. Despite the rain, Jim's spirits rose as he ate his cone: To a Swedish-Finnish Minnesotan, where there is ice, there is hope.

Suddenly, some open Army trucks splashed up alongside the sailors; brakes squealed; someone barked an order to climb aboard. Jim threw his sea bag up and scrambled in behind it, wondering what business seamen had with the Army. The caravan headed inland, into the steaming jungle, away from the ice cream, through the rain. It went on for miles and miles, and Jim's spirits became as soggy as his drenched sea bag.

Three Japanese groups had occupied this island: the Kembu Group, the Shobu Group and the Shimbu Group. The Kembu Group, controlling Manila, Manila Bay, Corregidor and the nearby Bataan Peninsula, was defeated, and those areas were firmly under American control. Jim's caravan was headed toward the territory of the other two groups.

They arrived at an Army base and were directed to their new quarters, tents with wooden floors. They were about 60 miles inland. *Inland! What the heck?* Jim went to his chief.

"Hey chief, where's the water? I thought I joined the Navy!"

The chief shrugged his shoulders. "The Navy doesn't seem to know what to do with us," he said. "So we're just going to stay here and do Army house-keeping until they got it figured out. You want water, you'll have to make do with the stuff that's falling on us."

There was plenty of that. So much, in fact, that Jim didn't see enough sunlight to get his directions straightened out, and never did learn just where the base was on that island. It appeared to be a temporary base, where "high-point men" were gathering to be sent home.

"High-point men" were those who quali-fied for discharge under the Army's new Adjusted Service Rating Plan. It was established shortly after

Germany's surrender, and awarded soldiers points based on time in service, time overseas, decorations, campaigns and dependent children. Eighty-five points won the soldier a trip home.

Jim watched the high-point men drift in from the battle zones. Some were wounded; many were sick; all suffered battle fatigue, which in a future war would be called post-traumatic stress syndrome. Jim felt ashamed that he ever had complained about anything - not only in the Navy, but in his whole life.

Sixty years later, remembering these soldiers, Jim choked up, and his eyes filled with tears. "Those men - I can still see their faces. If you put your hand up in front of their eyes, they wouldn't blink. No recognition at all...I can still see their faces."

Just as the chief said, the seamen were put to keeping house for the Army, preparing food, washing dishes, cleaning toilets. As Jim was doing dishes one especially sultry evening, he heard a rustling out in back, where the garbage was. Thinking it might be some sort of interesting tropical wildlife, he went out to have a look. A half dozen skinny Filipino kids and a few men were hauling garbage out of the barrels and dumping it into buckets. They cast him wary but friendly looks.

"Well, hi there," he said.

They nodded, said something in a language he didn't understand, and continued filling their buckets.

Then they left, disappearing down a path into the jungle.

For days, Jim wondered about them. Were they eating this stuff themselves, or feeding it to pigs? He decided to find out. He followed the path, which led through an area that had so far escaped deforestation. Huge mahogany trees rose out of sight, draped with lianas. Strangler fig vines dripped from breadfruit and mamey trees. High in the hardwood branches grew orchids and ferns. He passed a magnificent mango tree, its pendulous fruit still green. He could hear monkeys calling one another; the raucous cry of a parrot. It was hard to believe anyone could be poor here, or angry enough to stage a war.

By then, the Shimbu Group, like the Kembu Group, had all but disappeared as a fighting force for Japan. The Shobu Group continued undefeated; not as an attack force, but just trying to survive. Fighting continued in different pockets on the island. Jim suddenly realized that a Japanese sniper could be sitting incongruously among these flowers and vines at this very moment, his rifle aimed at Jim's unhelmeted head. The thought made him hurry a little, and he soon came to a clearing. And there was the village, an assortment of bamboo homes high on stilts, with chickens and pigs and half-naked children scampering around beneath. A group of adults had gathered in the village center. They looked at him appraisingly. Then several smiled and motioned for him to join them. He walked toward the group, skirting a water buffalo - some called them Philippines caribou - lying in a mud puddle. Her muddy udder was full.

That ice cream must have come from caribou cream,
he thought disconnectedly. The group was circled
around a plain wooden box that held a dead man. Jim
had come upon a funeral.

A ceremony followed, and then a fast trot to a
burial ground; the casket bounced on the shoulders
of the bearers. Later there was a feast. None of the
food looked like it had come from the garbage at the
base. There were bananas and other fruit he didn't
recognize; dishes of mashed sweet potato; roasted
pork; chicken cooked with Filipino beans; and some
kind of grilled meat that might be snake or lizard, or
maybe monkey. It looked and smelled inviting, but
Jim was due back in the kitchen, and he left, thanking
them in sign language.

A week later, Jim was bringing trays of sausage
and powder-mix scrambled eggs to the chow line,
when he heard the news: MacArthur had announced
that the Philippines had been liberated. The gaunt
infantry faces in the line registered no joy. One
vacant-eyed soldier commented wearily: "Yeah, the
Japs are gone. Must'a been a tree that shot Cummings
this morning."

That night Jim went through his nightly ritual
of tucking the bug netting tightly around his bunk,
to keep the insect multitudes out. He thought about
Cummings, the private who had died that day, and
the Shobu snipers who kept on fighting. He watched
a couple of black widow spiders scramble across the
netting, as though searching for an entrance to attack
him. He began to doze off. *Jap spiders Jap snipers
Jap spiders Jap snipers…*

"HEY!" Frenchy's frantic voice burst into his brain. Jim leaped up, tangling himself in the net, confusedly looking for the Jap sniper who had been lurking at the edge of his dreams. Despite the confusion, he glimpsed the figure of a man near his bunk; the man held a knife raised high. The dark figure turned, dropped the knife and fled. Frenchy emerged from the netting of the next bunk. "Man, Jim, that guy was going to kill you!" he gasped. A few other tent mates were up by now, and they searched the area unsuccessfully.

"What the heck?" Jim said, as they settled back into their bunks. "First on the ship, now here! If I'm going to get killed in this war, it oughta be a Jap with a bomb, not somebody on our side with a knife!"

"How do you know he was on our side?" Frenchy asked. The knife was Marine issue. Jim kept it. They never did learn who the attacker was.

The sailors remained at the Army base through July. On the 16th, the United States made its first atomic bomb test at Alamagordo, New Mexico. On the 24th, a destroyer escort, the *USS Underhill*, was hit by a piloted torpedo off Luzon.

"Nah, that was no torpedo," one of the sailors joked, as he cut up some tough Australian beef for a soup. "The war here is over. That ship must'a got hit by the same damn tree that got Cummings."

On a night in early August, the chief stopped by each tent and told the half-sleeping men inside they would be moving out in the morning. Their new home would be the *USS Rigel*, a repair ship anchored in Manila Harbor.

The 424-foot-long *Rigel* had been a tender - a supply ship - for destroyers and had been in Pearl Harbor during the Japanese attack. She had been only slightly damaged, and her crew had worked on rescue operations. She then was fitted with four 3-inch guns and saw action in Guadalcanal and in the attack on Leyte Gulf. The ship earned 4 stars and had been in the Philippines since January.

It was good to be back on a ship, even if it didn't seem to be going anywhere; and it was good to do the work he had been trained for. As a motor mechanic third class, Jim was among those responsible for all the small craft on the ship. They repaired and over-hauled the inboard engines, and kept the vessels painted and shipshape. His job was also to operate the 50-foot motor launch, taking the crew to shore for their liberty time - first those from port side, then those from starboard. It was an open launch, with seats all the way across, and Jim operated the engine. The boatswain, who operated the rudder, would use bells to signal Jim what to do next. The returns from liberty could be exciting; the men often were drunk and had to be poured into the launch like wet noodles. Often fights erupted, and the men ended up in the brig.

Not long after their move to the *Rigel*, they heard that a new and devastating bomb had been dropped on Japan. A couple of days later word was passed that another atomic bomb had been dropped. And a few days after that came the big news: Japan had surrendered. A celebration erupted, Americans and Filipinos shouting and firing off guns and fireworks.

The whole bay lit up with the display. *Bud's okay now*, Jim thought. *He can go home*. And then he thought: *I can go home too!*

But things move slowly with the military. It was months before the *Rigel* would get underway, and more than a year before Jim would get his discharge. In the meantime, the sailors kept the *Rigel* ship-shape and found ways to spend their free time.

"Jim, you want to go on an excursion with us, maybe get some souvenirs?" a buddy asked one day.

"Sure. Where?"

"The Rock."

The "Rock" was Corregidor, an island of less than a square mile that guarded the entrance to Manila Harbor. Six months earlier, 4,000 Japanese had died there, not counting thousands more thought to have blown themselves up in underground tunnels and others who drowned while swimming away from the island. Because the ground attack on Corregidor had been preceded by shelling from the sea and bombing from the air (more than 2,000 successful sorties, dropping more than 3,000 tons of bombs), American casualties were only 667. The U.S. dead and wounded had been removed, but the 4,000 Japanese bodies remained.

Waves battered the launch as the small group of sightseeing sailors made its way to the Rock. From a distance, Corregidor looked like a barren, uninteresting volcanic island.

Up close it looked more like a nightmare. The odor of spoiled meat hit them first, before their brains could comprehend the meaning of all those bodies. Rotting corpses, draped in rotting uniforms, lay everywhere, with grenades and other ammo scattered among them. Jim stepped over one body, around another. There were so many it was hard not to step on anyone. Every so often he could picture a face, the way it probably was before insects, carrion eaters or decay had attacked it. Young, like him. They were all young, like him. Caught in something bigger, and not knowing why. He was one young guy who could hardly move a foot without stepping on the corpses of other young guys, the results of war. Anger flooded him.

Those politicians. Those politicians, he thought furiously. *They sit in their safe offices and they make this happen. I'd like to rub their noses in this. I'd like to have them right here, and rub their noses in it.*

Back in the launch, no one said a word. They sat in shocked, solemn silence all the way back to the ship.

Thanksgiving passed. Then Christmas. Then Jim's 18th birthday. March was almost spent, when orders came to pull out. *Weighing anchor for the last time*, Jim thought. *Oakland is straight ahead.*

But the Pacific had other ideas. A typhoon wound through the southern Pacific in early April, and the *Rigel* hit the tail of it. That "tail" comprised the worst storm Jim could have imagined. The *Rigel* climbed high waves and plunged into troughs. Violent waves charged over the bow of the ship, causing panic in some of the crew. "You think this is bad!" the boatswain shouted. "You oughta sail on Lake Superior!"

Lake Superior was only 30 miles from Cloquet; Jim doubted that the familiar inland sea could be treacherous.

For days, the *Rigel* rolled from side to side. It made almost no headway. No one could go top side; work virtually came to halt; the store of steel in the machine shop clanged so loudly that ears stopped working.

Finally the storm abated. No one had been injured and no serious damage had been done, but repairs were needed: The propeller shaft had been damaged and some hull plates were bulging. The *Rigel* changed course and sailed to Midway Island for repairs.

During the week's wait, Jim explored the little sand island. It was there he saw his first live Japanese. They were behind a fence in a POW camp. One prisoner had a huge red Japanese flag tattooed all the way across his back. Jim noticed that some of the U.S. guards acted very harshly toward the prisoners - taunting them, pushing them around, swearing at them. Although he understood why - some of these Americans had gone through hell, fighting for their lives - he still felt compassion for the prisoners, just as he had for the dead men on Corregidor, and for the shellshocked GI s back in the Army camp. Most were just victims of circumstance, who wanted to serve their country too, he thought. He was glad to see that some American guards treated the prisoners decently, and that the Japanese seemed to be healthy.

Many people hated the Japanese, but I never did. Maybe because I was raised to have compassion. My dad, even with his drinking problems, had compassion for people, especially needy children. My mother and grandmother never turned anyone away from the home. No matter who they were, if they needed food or comfort, they got it. My grandmother always said that a stranger at your door might be an angel in disguise.

As it turned out, prisoners in American camps fared rather well; an estimated 95 percent of Japanese POWs survived the war, compared with less than half of allied POWs (Americans, Filipinos, Australians, English, Dutch and others) who had been in Japanese camps.

The *Rigel's* repairs completed, they headed toward California. Although the ocean provided no more stormy excitement, a crewman did. Luke Waters, a North Carolinian, was a gambler with a violent streak and a grudge against the captain's cat. He had been plotting how to throw the cat overboard ever since Manila. Back in the Philippines, he used to smuggle whiskey aboard, organize crap games and get in fights. Jim had always avoided the crap games - mostly because of the admonitions from home against gambling, but also because Waters seemed unbalanced. Luke bragged that someday the crew would see his name in print: "Wanted, Luke Waters, for murder."

Now, as the ship neared California, Jim happened by one of Waters' crap games. Waters had a soup bowl full of whiskey and a pile of money in front of him. Jim's buddy, Rich Sabol, was playing, too

"Get in the game, Esala," Waters growled. It wasn't a question, but an order.

"Nope."

"C'mon, Jim, shoot craps with us," Sabol asked nervously. He could see Waters was up to something.

"Nope."

Waters jumped to his feet, his eyes shining crazily. He looked around for fight-bait; pointed at the ceiling.

"Do you think I can jump so high that I can get my feet on the overhead?" he asked.

"Nope."

Waters erupted. He charged Jim like a wild man, tipping the whiskey bowl and scattering the money. Jim jumped out of the way, then ran as Waters continued after him. He chased Jim around the ship, picking up a meat cleaver as they raced through the galley. Jim ran even faster then, and got away. He stayed away until his own temper cooled.

"Man!" Jim later said to Frenchy and Sabol. "I sure hope I survive peacetime!"

The next time he saw Waters, the captain's cat had disappeared and the gambler was in the brig. Jim had pulled KP duty and had to bring Waters his food tray. The cook warned him to be careful; even from behind bars the man was giving everybody a hard time. *Let him try,* Jim thought hopefully, as he approached Waters' cell. *He tries to mess with me, he'll get his grub by air.* As soon as Waters saw Jim coming, he pulled the wooden end piece off his cot, stuck it through the bars and tried to poke the tray out of Jim's hands. Jim stepped back, grinning, and transferred the tray to the palm of his right hand. Waters swore and stretched toward him, his shoulder tight against the bars, waving the stick. Jim blocked the stick, and with the move of a pie-throwing contestant, slammed the tray flat against the bars. The food catapulted in and splattered Waters; hot mashed potatoes and gravy dripped down his face, pudding clung to his shirt, meat balls dropped to the floor. "Enjoy your dinner, jailbird," Jim called as he left the brig.

He never saw Waters again.

The *Rigel* sailed under the Golden Gate and into the bay. Back in the USA at last. *Back to peace. Back to Cloquet,* Jim thought.

Wrong on both counts. There was a prison riot in progress on Alcatraz Island. And, for reasons unrelated to the riot, the *Rigel* crew wouldn't be mustered out for two more months.

Jim and Frenchy went up to the captain's area, and aimed the powerful telescope at Alcatraz. They could see the small war there. People were scurrying all around. Puffs of dust and smoke dotted the air. The riot lasted two days.

Their mail caught up with them, and a letter from home said that Bud would be in San Francisco in May. It was already May. Jim's heart leaped. *Hey! Maybe he's already here!* He asked around; sure enough, his brother was on shore, in the city, right now. He tried to communicate with him from the *Rigel*, but had no luck. So he got shore leave and went searching. He'd see the back of a tall sailor about Bud's size, and rush up to him, look eagerly into his face - and see a stranger. Bud was nowhere to be found. It felt sadly familiar, to be so near his brother after three years of war, and yet blocked from seeing him - kind of like their childhood in Cloquet.

On Market Street, he ran into a buddy from the ship. Deciding they weren't presentable in their worn-out Navy issue clothing, they bought tailor-made uniforms. Looking sharp, they sauntered down the street, which was noisy and colorful with bars, penny arcades and prostitutes. Jim drank a few beers with his buddy, played some arcade games and exchanged insults with several Marines. He declined the ladies of the night, however.

> *I think the prayers of my mother and grandmother guarded me through all those temptations. You know, the Bible says to raise up a child in the way he should go, and he shall not depart from it as a man. That must be the way it worked with me.*

Jim's pal, a tough guy from the East Coast, was looking for a fight. As he swaggered down the street, he refused to salute passing officers. "I'd rather punch them in the nose," he declared. He threw around so many insults in Chinatown that he eventually created a brawl, and Jim had to join in to keep his friend from getting pounded. Military police were called to the scene, and that night, Jim and his belligerent buddy slept in the brig.

*   *   *

Knives, a cleaver - and now sharks. Jim's daily routine while the *Rigel* was anchored in the bay was to haul men in the 50-foot motor launch from the ship to shore and back. That meant he and other crew members had to climb out over shark-infested water on a rope leading to the 25-foot-long outrigger, then walk along its six-inches of diameter out to the Jacob's ladder, weave their way down as they swung in the breeze, and then move along the tiedown that cabled the launch to the ship. No life jackets were used or necessary; the sharks, clearly visible below, wouldn't let anyone drown. It was a frightening procedure every time, and Jim seriously began to wonder if he would ever get home.

Then came a day in July when the *Rigel* was decommissioned, and her crew could go home - all except two. Jim and another of his buddies, a Pennsylvanian named Spinner, had been given one last job, which would last until October. They had to help take the *USS Catalpa* to the "Boneyard" in Oregon for decommissioning. The *Catalpa* was a "net layer," meaning she spent the war laying surface-to-bottom netting of interlocking steel rings across bays and harbors to prevent enemy submarines from getting through. She had two battle stars for World War II service. She was to be laid up at the Pacific Reserve Fleet, in Astoria, Oregon, also known as the Boneyard. That meant the ship, guns and all, would be wrapped in plastic - what the Navy already was calling "shrink-wrap" - and kept ready for emergency recommissioning (in fact, she was commissioned again, for the Korean war).

The trip to Oregon started by heading 60 miles out to sea, and then turning up the coast. The land swells were huge, the going was rough. Once again, the pins on the nautical map seemed hardly to move at all. *Boy, am I ever going to get out of the Navy?* Jim thought.

But when they arrived at the Columbia River, the trip turned idyllic. As they moved upriver, they enjoyed calm, sunny weather and the slowly moving vistas of evergreens and willows, so like that of northern Minnesota. The *Catalpa* delivered, Jim and Spinner bid goodbye and got on their separate buses.

In Minneapolis, Jim was mustered out, and given the insignia servicemen called the "ruptured duck," a golden label showing an eagle inside a wreath. The insignia was proof that the bearer had been discharged honorably, was not AWOL, and had the right to wear the uniform for the next month.

As he sewed the golden label onto the right breast pocket of his tailor-made uniform, he thought about the months he had just spent while earning this insignia. He felt good. He had done all right. He had served his country, and he hadn't had to kill anyone.

Then he shouldered his bag and headed for home.

*That which is false troubles the heart, but truth
brings joyous tranquility.*

- Jalaluddin Rumi

CHAPTER 6

Joy

It is a grey fall day, but the yellow maple leaves
strewn across the parking lot of Northland Funeral
Home lend a golden glow to the air. I have come to
this place to hear Jim preach a funeral.

June's.

The cheerful singing lady has passed on, and
the funeral home is filling up rapidly. Soon there is
standing room only in the large room with the casket
and the pulpit in the front. Jim's wife Chery, who is
June's daughter, is standing near the casket, looking
forlorn and grief-stricken. Others of June's children,
grandchildren and great-grandchildren file past. She
had a big family, and evidently a caring one. Even
some of the young children are crying.

Jim's voice is sure and strong as he addresses
the group. He talks about June and her fun-loving

ways; about the trips out west they all took together, and about their trip to Sweden, along with Jim's own mother. In the manner of evangelical preachers, his funeral address includes a call to salvation. There are a few frowns and a bit of restlessness among some mourners who perhaps didn't expect to be proselytized.

Jim doesn't concern himself with defining and dissecting the doctrine of salvation: *Justification/ participation. Whether God planned the fall from grace, or merely allowed it to happen. Faith versus works.* His approach is simple and direct. Salvation is being saved. Saved from misery and death. Carried into the eternal joy of knowing God. Salvation is walking with Jesus from unhappiness to happiness. What's so hard to understand? If you're relaxing in a chair, must you analyze intellectually whether the chair *really* exists?

My mind begins wandering, and I think about something I just read, a true anecdote about the philosopher Morris Cohen:

Cohen's college class had been probing the nature of reality. After class one day, a student stopped him.

"Professor," he said in an anguished voice, "I feel terrible!"

"How so?" Cohen asked.

"I don't know who I am!" the student wailed. "Do I really exist?"

Cohen looked searchingly into the eyes of the skinny boy. He smiled; his eyes twinkled.

"Hmm," he said. "So... Who wants to know?"

I giggle out loud and then, embarrassed, pretend to cough. Fortunately, it appears that no one noticed my interruption. I force my thoughts back to the service.

Jim is telling us that June was "saved." I wonder if what he means by that would be exactly what she might have thought - or even what his prayer partners think. Then he says that June is now "with the Lord." Again, I wonder what exactly he means by that. What do any of us imagine when we use such terms - or words like God and Faith? How do we know we're all on the same page? And does it matter?

The so-called "perennial philosophers" probably would say it doesn't. The human yearning for the divine, they say, is universal, and the world's religions are only cultural spins on the same essential elements: that the truest part of our selves is spiritual; that in engaging that spark of spirit, we can divinely and intuitively know God; and that unity with the Divine is the chief end of human existence. They say —

Oops, my mind is wandering again. I bring it back to the service, which Jim is keeping simple.

Afterwards, we move into the Fireside Room, where an abundant lunch is being served. Nearby is the photo table. Chery arranged it, and in the center is her photo portrait of her mother. The table is spread with unadorned oak leaves, a tribute to June's simplicity and her love of nature. The portrait shows June wearing a modest cotton smock and a big smile against a backdrop of trees. It exactly catches her joyfulness.

I glance at Jim, who is sitting at a table, visiting with others. Despite his sorrow, he too has a joyful demeanor: the joyful tranquility of the Jalaluddin Rumi poem.

Rumi said falsehood troubles the heart. Clearly, Jim's heart, though grieving, is untroubled.

*   *   *

On another day, I ask Jim about tranquility. "People are so tired of falseness," he says, unwittingly touching precisely on Rumi's point. "They're tired of the show of personality, tired of the show of how much money someone's got. When the only thing that matters is love.

"You know, the greatest commandment that God gave is to love one another."

We have given up our personal desires so that our will is merged with God's own will....in his will is our peace: it is the sea into which all currents and all streams empty themselves, for all eternity.

- Dante Alighieri

CHAPTER 7

Home is the Sailor, Home from the Sea

There had been no special homecoming - no party, no guest-of-honor dinner, no "welcome back" signs. The waves of returning veterans had diminished months ago, and the ardor of welcome with them. At home, Jim's family wasn't the kind to make a fuss, although everyone, possibly even Gramps, was relieved and grateful he was home from the war, safe and sound.

Knowing his undemonstrative family, he hadn't expected anyone to meet him at the train station in Duluth. But there was Bud, grinning a welcome. Overjoyed, Jim rushed up to him and shook his hand. "Man, I looked all over Frisco for you!" he exclaimed.

They stopped at a tavern, where Bud brought him up to date on the home front: He had found work fixing electrical appliances; Mom and Grandma were still praying up a storm; Dad was still drinking, but had a job in Duluth working at a greenhouse; Gramps was still Gramps. That Greek girl was dating some Greek guy in Duluth. There wasn't a fair this year.

"Why not?"

"Polio. Well, first the fairgrounds got hit by a tornado. Most of the buildings are gone. All those pines, too. They hurried up and got it halfway cleaned up and were going to have the fair anyway, and then some people got polio, so they had to cancel it."

Jim pictured the county fairgrounds in Barnum: white clapboard buildings, a horse race track, a grove of big pines; young people exhibiting their sheep and calves and preserves. "I guess the 4-H kids took their stuff down to St. Paul anyway."

"Nope. No state fair either, on account of polio."

Jim had difficulty focusing on fairs and polio as he studied his brother's face. Bud looked different somehow - older, of course, like he himself probably looked older - but several times he caught an expression resting in the background of his brother's countenance that reminded him of the high-point infantry men on Luzon.

Eventually Bud wound up the news from home, and the brothers fell silent. They finished their beers and Bud indicated to the bartender to bring them seconds.

"What was it like?" Jim said.

"What?"

"You know - the war. What was it like for you? You didn't write much about it."

Bud shrugged casually, but his face looked like a door had shut. "Like anybody else, I guess." He drained his glass. "How about another beer?"

Like anybody else? It seemed to Jim that every man's experience was different. He knew he had been extraordinarily lucky to have come into the war just as it was ending. Bud had been there through the worst of it. Jim took a swallow of the third beer the bartender had slid in front of him and glanced at his brother, who was studying the bottles in back of the bar. "No, I mean - You didn't say much in your letters - Was your LCT ever hit? Did you have to kill anybody? Did any of your buddies get hurt?"

Bud made a gesture of dismissal. "I don't want to talk about all that. It's in the past now. Just forget it."

Jim decided to ask him another time, when Bud gave him an opening. But Bud never did.

*   *   *

At home, Dad greeted him with a handshake and a gruff, "So you're back."

Mom, her eyes shining, handed him a package. "Your father and I got you something."

Jim opened it: a hand-knit sweater, with the design of a Lockheed P-38 lightning fighter plane knitted right into it. The P-38 had shot down more

Japanese planes in the war than any other fighter. It was the plane Major Richard Ira Bong - who was practically their neighbor, since he hailed from Poplar, Wisconsin, only 50 miles away - had piloted when he won his Congressional Medal of Honor.

It was beautiful, and Jim was touched. "Thanks."

*   *   *

The men who returned ahead of him had grabbed all the jobs, it seemed to Jim. He looked all winter and couldn't find work anywhere.

"Hey, I've got an idea," Bud said. "Remember Walt Broman?"

Of course Jim remembered Walt Broman. He was a contractor whose home the brothers had visited when they were boys and attended youth meetings at Lakeview Covenant Church in Duluth. Walt's sons attended too, and Walt often had the group over to his house for treats and socializing later.

"What about him?"

"Jerry mentioned the other day that his dad put in a bid on some big project out in North Dakota. If he lands it, I bet he'll hire you."

The "big project" turned out to be the Garrison Dam. Broman did get the contract, and Jim did get the job, and that spring he drove to Underwood, North Dakota. When he pulled onto the wide muddy main street, he found the town buzzing like a Wild West gold camp. Cars, trucks and pedestrians hummed past the false-front wooden buildings. The town was busy with a growing pool of construction workers who had come to build the 12,000-foot dam across the Missouri River. The dam would be made of earth piled 210 feet high.

Underwood was flat and Main Street was tree-less, and it looked a little dismal to Jim - so plain compared to the hills and woods at home. The sky went on forever. The dam site was 20 miles away, where caterpillars, bulldozers and scrapers were moving dirt 24 hours a day. Not far from there, on a bluff on the east side of the river, a new town was being built. Riverdale would house dam officials and employees after the dam was operative; it was built on a half-wheel design, with the hub the offices of the Army Corps of Engineers, and the spokes the streets. Broman was a subcontractor installing water lines and sewers for the new town.

Boom towns - Big Bend, Sitka, Dakota City, Pick City, Silver City - were popping up between Underwood and the dam site. They were more like shanty towns, and accommodated the increasing work population with bars, tar-paper shack cafes and dancing girls. Granaries from the farms that would be flooded were moved to the new towns for workers' quarters, and Jim moved into one.

His initial job was hauling cement sewer tile to the townsite. He had an elderly helper named Wimpy, a local man with a white beard and a debilitating hernia. Wimpy's clothing was raggedy and dirty; he never spoke of family or friends; he seemed to be always hungry. Jim felt sorry for him.

One morning in the mess hall, Jim was watching Wimpy pile his plate high with flapjacks while half listening to a conversation at the next table: a cement worker named Les was commenting about how many goody-goody contractors were on this job. "They pray before meals, they pray before they go to bed, they even meet for prayers at lunchtime," he said to the man near him.

"Like who?" the other man asked.

"Let's see: the guy working on pipe in - hey Jim!" Les called.

Wimpy slathered butter between every pancake on his stack. Jim pulled his eyes from Wimpy's plate and turned toward Les at the next table.

"What's the name of the guy you work for?"

"Broman." Jim turned his attention back to Wimpy; the old man had used the entire chunk of butter from one of the common butter dishes.

"That's him. Then there's the guy he subs for - Jim?"

Wimpy was pouring on the syrup now. He used more than half the pitcher. "Ken Erickson. Standard Construction," Jim answered, without looking at Les. He wondered that Wimpy didn't get sick with all that fat and sugar.

"Yeah. Then there's LeTourneau, big outfit from Duluth," Les told the other man. "Hell, they're all from Duluth."

"Maybe you should pray too, Les!" the other man said. "Those guys got rich on it!"

"I guess so," Les replied. "You're not going to believe this - That LeTourneau? He gives his money away. They say he gives away 90 percent - *90 percent* - of everything he makes, and he only keeps 10."

"You're right, I don't believe it."

With deliberation, Wimpy began eating: first the top pancake, then the second. He worked his way slowly to the bottom until the plate was clean. The little old man put away twice as many pancakes as 19-year-old Jim, 6 feet and still growing

One evening after work, Wimpy began walking home as usual. His feet seemed to drag more than on other days; his hernia had been bothering him all afternoon. At one point during the day, Jim had been forced to stop the truck so Wimpy could stretch out on the ground and push his hernia back into place.

"How about a ride, Wimpy?" Jim asked.

"I'd surely appreciate that," the old man said tiredly, and climbed into Jim's Ford pickup.

Wimpy pointed toward the river. They went down the road a way and then the old man gestured toward a path. Jim turned the wheel. The scenery was nice here; the cottonwoods were thick, and the settled old earth was a relief from the raw scraped ground of the new towns and construction sites. They bumped along to the riverbank. The water below was muddy. There wasn't a house in sight.

"Here," Wimpy said.

Jim stopped. "Where?"

"Right here. My place is below the bank."

Jim got out and followed him. Wimpy walked down a small path over the edge of the riverbank, and stopped in front of a cave. "This is it. Home sweet home."

An animal skin was hanging over the entrance. Inside the dark hole was a ring of rocks - Wimpy's fireplace.

"This is where you live?" Jim asked, unbelievingly. The place made the Army base on Luzon look like a luxury resort.

"Yup."

"How long you been living here?"

"Couple months, since the government kicked me off my place. It's going under water, soon's the dam's done."

Jim left Wimpy and returned to camp. There, he ran into a co-worker friend, Mike. Mike was a "Eucskinner" - the operator of a Euclid earth-mover. Jim had watched him up there under the Euclid's canvas awning, working the controls and moving 50 yards of dirt in a single scoop. It was an impressive machine and looked fun to operate.

The pair decided to go to the Silver Dollar and then hit all nine bars in nearby Big Bend. The Silver Dollar was loud and crowded as usual. Two dancing girls who worked in one of the other boom towns sat at a table, drinking but minding their own off-duty business.

Jim told Mike about Wimpy and the cave. "I feel bad about him," he said. "That sick old man in a cold cave…"

"I'll talk to the boss," Mike said. "He's a pretty good guy. He could maybe get him a bunk over on the other side."

"Who's your boss?"

"LeTourneau."

Just then Jim noticed two local guys moving in on the girls' table. One of the boys was acting aggressive. The girls tried to ignore him, but he persisted;

he raised his voice; soon he was using foul language. Jim couldn't stand bad language in front of women. His temper flared and suddenly he was itching for a fight. He strode over to the man and tapped him on his shoulder. "Hey, big shot."

The man spun around, turning angry eyes on him.

Jim's growing talent for sarcasm blossomed when watered by beer, and he'd already had two. "Oh, he's mad, the little rooster crowing stupid in front of women," he sneered. "You got anything stronger than bad-boy words, big shot?"

In the fight that ensued outdoors, the man got a tight grip on Jim's P-38 sweater. He pulled and twisted at the plane design until the yarn threads started popping, and no matter how Jim wrestled and slugged him, he wouldn't let go until it was ripped out of the sweater. Jim's fist helped him in his downward fall, and he was out.

Jim was steaming mad about his sweater when he took off, leaving the local guy stretched out on the ground. He forgot all about the plans he and Mike had for the evening. It wasn't until he was already in bed that he thought of a name: LeTourneau. *A praying man, gives away his money, would care about somebody like Wimpy.* The picture made him uncomfortable. He was reflecting on the qualities of faith and commitment and compassion - and feeling somewhat guilty about his temper - when he dozed off.

Once all the pipe was hauled, Jim was put to work with a water pipe laying crew. The pipefitters laid six-inch steel pipe along the bottom of a ditch and started connections by putting a snap ring made of hard fiber around the pipe's bell joint. They packed it with oakum and poured hot lead into the joint; as soon as the lead set, they removed the snap ring and punched the lead tightly into the bell joint, and moved on to the next connection.

Jim's job was to heat the lead in a kettle over a wood fire. A plumber named Swede, who was from Holyoke near Cloquet, showed Jim how to heat the lead to the right temperature. When a wood splinter flamed up immediately when dropped into the hot liquid, the lead was ready. Jim then ladled the lead into a bucket, brought it to the edge of the six-foot-deep ditch, and handed it down to the pipefitters. Every so often he had a horrifying picture of what would happen should he spill the bucket. The acute concern made him tense.

He worked off his tension at lunchtime. A new water tower had been erected for the town-to-be, and he climbed up the ladder and then crawled out over the top of the tank. He could see a long way from up there; the ditches below looked like scratches in the ground, the mounds of earth at the distant dam site like cow pies. The next time he went up, he took along a camera.

They finished the job in late autumn, and Jim was laid off. On the way home, he thought of the remark the *Rigel* boatswain had made about Lake Superior. *Lake Superior as bad as a Pacific typhoon?* Jim decided to see for himself. He drove into Duluth and joined the merchant marine.

A week later, he shipped out of Ashland, Wisconsin, on the *Sweden*, a 434-foot steamer that was loaded with grain. The boat looked to Jim more like a barge than a ship. But once under way, rolling deck and grinding engines, a body of water reaching to the horizon, he felt like a sailor again. As a deck hand, he was on call around the clock. He didn't mind the work, and he relished the meals: three big home cooked feasts and good chuck left out all night for the nighttime hands.

After several hundred uneventful miles, the *Sweden* arrived at Sault Ste. Marie. There they entered a lock system that bypassed the falls and rapids of the St. Mary's River, a 60-mile-long waterway connecting Lake Superior with Lake Huron. It was Jim's first sight of Canada, and he found the "Soo" locks fascinating; millions of gallons of water pouring out of a lock in a matter of minutes, and the whole ship slowly dropping, lock by lock, until it was 20 feet lower and at the level of Lake Huron. Another 200 miles across Lake Huron, and the *Sweden* entered the 89-mile-long river channel connecting Huron with Lake Erie. With only an 8-foot drop to Erie, no lock was necessary. The trip downriver was crowded with ships and offered a good view of Detroit. They unloaded the wheat at Sandusky, Ohio, and Jim went looking for an upbound ship. He found it: the 500-foot *Ball Brothers*, taking on a load of coal. He walked up the gangplank and signed on.

Back up the chain: same trip in reverse. This time they bypassed Ashland and headed directly for the Duluth-Superior harbor. They anchored outside the

Duluth entrance alongside other ships awaiting their turn to go through the narrow canal, under the aerial bridge and into the bay. The crew passed some of the time on the *Marine Trader*, which tied up alongside. It was a "bum-boat" - a floating store carrying tobacco, work clothes, gloves, boots, pop, alcohol in pop cases, candy; and slot machines, which were legal in these international waters. As Jim descended the ladder into the bum-boat, he briefly considered that his descent toward alcohol and gambling might be viewed as symbolic.

Post-war wheat shipping was heavy, and all 20 grain elevators had ships standing open-hatched beside them. When the *Ball Brothers* finally got into the harbor and unloaded its cargo of coal, Jim and other deckhands had to sweep every inch of the hold. Jim moved along the high catwalks, brushing away soot with a fine brush. Their next cargo would be wheat, which inevitably heated up somewhat in transport; the heat could set coal residue afire and cause a deadly spontaneous combustion.

The boat was loaded by evening. It was calm when they left Duluth; a very slight southern breeze was warming the December air. Jim stood on the deck and looked out over the pink-tinted water toward the city skyline. The sun was sinking behind Duluth's high hills, and lights were coming on in the shadows below. It was a beautiful sight.

Sometime during the night, the wind switched to northeast. Jim, asleep in the bow of the boat, was awakened by the cold, and then a familiar yell: "Out of the bunk, you sea gulls, and hit the deck running!"

He and the other hands went out onto the rolling deck and grabbed the ropes to the safety cable. The cable stretched from bow to stern; attached to it were sliding rings with ropes hanging from them. They held onto the ropes or tied them around their waists as they worked: They checked the steel hatch covers, covering them tightly with canvas, driving in wooden pins to hold the canvas snug. The wheat below couldn't be allowed to get wet, and the waves were beginning to spray over the deck.

Back in his bunk, Jim was awakened for the second time when his foot locker bounced from the floor and crashed into the wall. He realized he was hungry. *I'd better go back and get something to eat before this gets worse,* he thought. His buddy, Al, had the same idea, and followed Jim out onto the deck.

It was dark, wind-sprayed, icy. The pitching and rolling were now severe; they tied the safety ropes to their waists and slowly made their way across the ice-covered deck back toward the galley. They bumped into someone: he was gripping the cable with both hands. It was a veteran crewman, Milt, so frozen with fear he couldn't reach for a rope or move down the cable. They got him hooked on and slipped and slid down to the galley, where the skipper gave them an angry reprimand for being out in that weather. Jim barely listened as he covered a slab of bread with butter and a thick slice of roast beef.

The wind had blown up some monster waves - not predictably spaced, like on the ocean, but choppy and chaotic. Waves crashing onto the deck soon coated the ship with ice. Headed into the wind, heavy with its icy blanket, the *Ball Brothers* struggled toward Canada.

About noon, she moved into the quieter waters of Port Arthur bay. The skipper announced that they would drop anchor there and wait out the storm.

That night as the men lay in their bunks, Al asked Milt why he had been so scared. Milt hadn't said a word about it, or about anything else since they had found him on the deck. He wasn't much of a talker anyhow; he seemed to have trouble making a whole sentence.

He paused awhile before answering. "Four years ago this very day. I was on another boat. Bound for this port. Never made it," he said.

"What boat?"

"The *Sarnian*."

"I heard about that!" a third crewman said. "She went down, right?"

"Uh-huh. Big northeast gale. Seventeen-foot waves. We got drove ashore in Bete Grise Bay, over on the Keweenaw Peninsula. Little ways south of Point Isabelle. Scared the hell out of me. Coast Guard rescued us."

The boat clanged and rocked and creaked. The men were silent awhile. "This lake's treacherous all right," the third man observed. "Thank God for the Coast Guard."

Jim, silent, thought: *Thank God, period.*

"What was that little packet that went down off Presque Isle a few months ago?" Al asked. "The one where the Coast Guard tug got grounded trying to save the guy on board?"

"Oh, yeah, that's the one the *Woodrush* got to before the waves broke it up. Got him out just in time." The men appreciated the 180-foot *Woodrush*. Built only four years earlier in Duluth, the Coast Guard cutter already had broken paths for many a laker stranded in the ice.

Then Al remembered: "The *Favorite*. It was the *Favorite*, that little packet that went down."

"That's it…"

Milt spoke up again. "All the lakes are dangerous," he said. "I knew a guy, maybe 10 years ago. Boat sunk in Lake Michigan. Right off the South Chicago lighthouse. Summertime even. Regular gale. Fifteen guys drowned. Maybe half a dozen made it. Boat's still down there. About 30 feet of water."

"Which one?"

"The *Material Service*."

"I heard about that," Al said. "They were stupid; she wasn't an open-water boat. She was only maybe half as long as this one, not made for the big lakes."

Stevens, an oiler, had been in the merchant marine 30 years, longer than any of the crew. "We like to think these big ones are made for them, but sometimes I wonder…take this boat we're on right now, the *Ball Brothers*. American Shipbuilding built her along with a bunch of others right around the same time, maybe 40 years ago. I knew a man shipped out on one, and she went down less than a month after she was built, only second trip out. Big storm, her cargo, iron ore I think it was, shifted and she turned turtle and sunk, all hands lost except for this one guy who told me about it. They were downbound from Superior, headed for Buffalo."

"What boat was that?"

"The *Cyprus*. Then around that time another American Shipbuilding boat went down. She was right in the middle of Lake Erie, in December like now, and in a gale, huge waves. They had a good sized crew, 30 or 40, and every man Jack of them died."

"You remember the name?"

"*Marquette and* ...something."

Milt was dozing off. "...we were carrying barley," he muttered.

"I sure hope American Shipbuilding ain't cursed," a fifth man said. "I'd like to get to Cleveland before Christmas."

They did, anchoring outside of Cleveland on December 23rd. The next day it was snowing, and Jim found himself standing on a swaying scaffold hanging off the stern, painting the hull. He was beginning to agree with the *Rigel* boatswain that the big lake's chop and cold made it more treacherous than the Pacific. On the typhoon-tossed *Rigel,* at least, his fingers weren't clumsy-numb and there was no ice on the deck to send him overboard.

They had finished unloading in Cleveland when Jim got a message that he should get home right away. His grandmother was seriously ill. He caught a bus for Cloquet, and his seafaring days were over.

*   *   *

High snow banks and stalled vehicles, frost on store windows and brown bundled figures hurrying to the next refuge. Downtown Cloquet in deep winter could be a forbidding place, and Jim had reason to drive through it often. Grandma's illness - the doctors didn't know exactly what was wrong - hospitalized her at Raiter Hospital several times. And Jim frequently drove his father to the older man's new job at the Wood Conversion plant.

Early February was unusually cold that year, but on Jim's 20th birthday, it suddenly turned very warm. Snowbanks were collapsing almost before his eyes. Sun-glistening water ran down the gutters. Spring! He felt a surge of happy energy, a sense of freedom and promise for the future. Then Grandma took a turn for the worse.

As Jim drove her through town, back to the hospital, he noticed people strolling on the sidewalks, looking vital and exuberant, freed from their homes and heavy overcoats, smiling at one another. He saw a pretty girl go by. He rolled down the window to see her better, to hear the voices of pedestrians, to feel the spring air.

"No, close it," Grandma said, shivering and adjusting her scarf.

"Sorry." He quickly closed it.

"It's good you're home again, Jim," she said weakly. "This is where you belong."

Her words gave him a sour feeling. Barricaded from the sunny warm day, he yearned for a free life as he yearned for an open window. He was glad to be able to help out, he loved his grandmother, but -

what about his own life? Didn't he have a right to get it under way? He wanted to see more of the world, settle into his own work, build his own family. He felt trapped.

The trapped feeling diminished in the evenings, when he and Bud and the Salmi brothers, Paul and Melvin, went out on the town. The four young men hit all the bars in the area: Glen's, Big Lake, Ken's, Archie's, the Rendezvous, Pine Lodge, the Green Top. They talked, they laughed, they drank, and three of them danced. Girls tried to get Jim to dance, but he absolutely refused. He knew women were attracted to him - he was now 6 feet, 1 inch, and had black curly hair they seemed to love - but he brushed them off. He didn't like their coy manipulative ways, the way they sidled up to him like he was their prey. He preferred to stay at the bar, and occasionally pick a fight by exercising his developing sarcastic wit. He was becoming known as a cocky character, someone who would deck a guy first and ask questions later.

Every so often someone would try to fix him up with a girl. "I can pick out my own girl," he growled. He felt certain that when the time was right, he'd meet the right woman for him, and he was pretty sure he wouldn't find her in a bar.

At Buck's Tavern in Scanlon one night, he met a man so tall that he had to look up to him. "I'm Herb," the man said. "We're cousins." Apparently fighting ran in the family. Herb soon picked one; Jim joined in to help his new cousin; a brawl ensued and Carlton County sheriff's deputies were called to the scene.

Both Jim and Herb were jailed for the night, and the Scanlon Police Chief visited them.

"We won't press charges as long as you never come through here again," he told them. "We're sick and tired of you Raleigh Street Boys looking for trouble down here."

The Raleigh Street Boys were a tough bunch from Duluth. When the chief learned that Jim was a local boy, he let him and his cousin go.

*   *   *

Gramps had been planning his garden all spring. Although he had retired from truck gardening, he still planted a large vegetable garden for their own use. He never bothered planting much before the end of May; late frosts were common this far north. Nevertheless, in early May, he told Jim to drive him to Roley's feed mill in Carlton for seeds, onion sets and seed potatoes.

The clapboard mill alongside the railroad track was a busy place, with clouds of grain dust billowing from the mill and farmers lined up at the dock loading calf feed and salt blocks and shiny aluminum watering tanks into their pickups. While Gramps picked out bulk seeds on the sales side of the building, Jim waited on the mill side. Stacks of gunny sacks bulging with grain crowded the wooden floor, and grayish flour coated every inch of wooden wall and rafter and post. The mill made as much noise as the *Ball Brothers'* engine. Jim enjoyed the sound and the yeasty smell of the grain.

John Nelson, a bachelor who sometimes stopped in for one of Mom's meals, came by carrying a grain sack on his shoulder. Like the other mill workers, he was covered with floury grain dust - hair, face, clothing, even his eyelashes. "How's your grandma?" he asked. "Heard she's back in the hospital."

"She's about the same. We're stopping by to see her on the way home," Jim replied. Just then Gramps summoned him to carry his purchases to the truck, and they left. Their route went through Scanlon.

"Pull in here," Gramps said, pointing at the Rendezvous. That was fine with Jim; a beer would clear away the grain dust from his throat.

He was always to regret that stop.

While Gramps and I were sitting in that tavern in Scanlon, Grandma died. She was in a hospital bed not two miles down the road from us. I felt bad about that for many years…. When you sow wild oats, you might not like the harvest you reap.

Elizabeth's grief was the grief of a young girl losing her only relative. It was as though her life and her world had ended; she fell silent and took to her bed. Jim knew Grandma had a huge impact on his mother - she did everything but breathe for her, he sometimes thought - but he never expected such a dramatic reaction.

Nine days after Grandma's death came the news that Israel had become a state. The happy news seemed to revive Elizabeth, and she called her family to her bedside. She told them that just before Grandma died she had elicited a promise from Elizabeth and made two prophecies. The promise was that Gramps would move into their home and Elizabeth would care for him as long as he lived -

"What?" Dad interrupted, aghast.

Using Grandma's authoritative gesture, Mom raised her hand to silence him, and continued: "The prophecies concern the boys. The first one is, 'Jim will be the first to return to the Lord; and Bud will follow later.' And the second one is, 'You aren't to worry, Elizabeth, because Jim will be here to take care of you.'"

Dad was furious and silent; Bud was inscrutable and silent; Jim was conflicted and silent. Was this more of Grandma's control? Had she arranged to manage, direct and manipulate every member of the family even after her death? He didn't want to doubt his grandmother or think ill of her, but - she wouldn't make this prophecy business up, would she? *No*, he concluded firmly. *But it could be she believed it came from God, when it really came from her own controlling spirit...*

None of them wanted Gramps living in their house; he and Dad still hated one another. Nevertheless, Gramps, age 77, reluctantly moved in, and Dad stayed away from home more than ever.

Jim stayed away too. Those prophecies were aggravating him; he hated being pushed into anything, and he decided that Grandma from her grave and Mom were pushing him into a corner from which there would be no exit for him. He passed summer evenings at the bars and getting into more fights.

That August, Bethany Church in Cloquet was hosting a series of guest preachers at special evening services. Mom wanted Jim to accompany her, and because she was still so sad and grieving, he went along. He always managed to slip out before anyone cornered him, though.

After one such meeting, he dropped his mother off at home and instead of driving down to Buck's Tavern as he planned, he just drove around. He felt restless. He had a nagging feeling that wouldn't go away. Something had been eating at him increasingly over the past few years.

As he drove aimlessly, he thought he knew what it was. He'd been on the fence: believing in God, but ignoring Him because he didn't want to cave in to Mom's and Grandma's expectations, and lose himself in a kind of swamp they seemed to have created for him.

But what if he set their expectations aside? Maybe he was meant to live in intimacy with the Lord. Maybe everybody was.

He turned onto the Ditchbank Road and pulled over at the top of a maple-covered hill. He turned off the engine and thought about his life. He sure wasn't happy with the way it was now - taverns, beer, cigarettes, bluffing, fighting, sarcasm; rushing from one mindless distraction to another, and never taking the time to pay attention. To listen to the still small voice.

He had heard it once, a long time ago, before he was old enough to know how to stay tuned in. It was the connection to the Lord, to His power and His love, and to all His children. When he was drinking or fighting, that connection didn't seem very important; it seemed tiny and distant and irrelevant. But really, what else could matter in life? Without that, what did anything matter?

Without it, he was adrift, a sailor alone on a dark and wild sea.

Maybe it's too late for me, he thought, and a tremendous sadness descended on him. Stunned with the intensity of the sorrow, he numbly started the engine, backed around and drove home. He didn't want to talk to anyone, so he slipped upstairs quietly. As he climbed the stairs, he felt a shifting of the weight on his heart and on his spirit. Instead of flopping onto his bed as he'd planned, he dropped to his knees beside it.

"Lord, I'm tired of all the sin in my life," he groaned. "Please forgive me and come into my heart."

It was that simple, that profound. The weight lifted, the storm abated, and the weary sailor dropped anchor.

Shirley

*A*lways a strong-headed child, Shirley now was maneuvering her own way between opposite expectations. At school, she was told she was required to learn, behave and produce. At home, there were no requirements. She didn't even have to feed herself; when she was 12, her mother still held her on her lap and fed her like a baby.

She was having trouble scholastically, but that didn't bother her. Her overprotective mother had trained her that she didn't have to do anything she didn't want to do, and she didn't like to study - so she didn't. She got through her classes anyway.

But she liked school. She had lots of friends; she loved to sing and dance; it was fun.

One by one, seven of her brothers and sisters had grown up and left home. Now only she and two sisters were left.

*Don't be afraid of people's sin. Love people even
in their sin, for it represents Divine love and is the
greatest love on Earth.*

- Father Zossima

CHAPTER 8

New Life

After that evening by his bedside, when Jim chose a life of intimacy with God, he never looked back. He hit detours and potholes along the way, but he stuck by the course that he, or perhaps God, had set.

His became a lifetime of caregiving. Caring for his alcohol-doomed father. Caring for neglected children. Caring for those who were hungry - bringing some people home to eat, and collecting day-old bakery goods and delivering them on a regular route. He cared for his mother, as she passed through stages of old age, blindness, cancer, death. He cared for June until her death in 2004.

And in between, he visited people - impromptu visits, sometimes to people he didn't know.

Consider: entering a stranger's hospital room, and just visiting. So simple, but so delicate; you must feel your way through, you must sense whether your presence is a help or a stress; you must be willing to sit in peaceful silence, simply sharing space together; you must listen.

Consider: knocking on the dirty, beat-up door of a troubled family, hearing screams inside. The door opening a crack, odors of beer and cigarette smoke and unwashed bodies, an angry face peering out; and behind it a drape-darkened room, the glare of a television, the sound of crying.

Consider: Stopping by a rural home and finding on the front lawn some rowdy drunken people watching a man trying to kill his brother with a scythe.

Consider: Pushing open the door of an apartment in response to a worried telephone plea, and finding a raped woman and her two drunken sons - the rapists.

What can one do in such situations?

"You just love them," Jim says. "You love all of them."

He doesn't mean that's all you do - stand by feeling love for people, as you watch them destroy one another. You also take action.

In the case of the murderous brother, Jim walked into the yard. His initial alarm was replaced by calm; he felt the assurance of heavenly protection.

"Who the hell do you think you are, white man?" someone in the crowd yelled. "This is Indian land, you damn pushy *chimoke*! Get the f— out of here!"

Ignoring him, Jim went over, placed himself between the fighters and told the man holding the scythe to put it down. Then someone from the crowd stepped forth, waving his wine bottle, and told everyone that Jim was a preacher and to leave him alone. The fight stopped; the crowd settled down. Inside the house Jim found three adults and two young children, all huddling in fear of the drunken chaos outside.

Jim visited the same home not long afterward to check on the murderous brother. Bill was having a rocky time of it. He had spent many years in prison, and when he got out, his beloved grandparents - respected elders on the reservation and part of Jim's prayer community - had died only a month apart. Bill was depressed and was isolating himself.

The house looked deserted in the twilight; Jim had a feeling that something was wrong. The dogs greeted him and he fed them long Johns and bismarcks from his bakery stash. Then he let himself into the house.

"Bill!" he called.

No answer. Jim went into the kitchen. A noise made him turn, to see a man leaping at him with a butcher knife ready to sink into his ribs. "Billy, it's me!" Jim yelled.

Bill threw up his hands, dropping the knife. "Oh my God!" he cried, and then lay his head on the table and began to weep. Jim ministered to him.

When he recalled the rape scene described above - this was a white household - Jim shook his head. "Oh, that was terrible, terrible. That poor family. I just wept when I saw their pain."

He ministered to them, too.

"You know, the Lord loves everyone - *everyone*. Who am I to feel differently? So I don't look at the bad things people do, the sins they commit. What I see is what they could be - what God wants them to be."

*   *   *

Early in this new phase of his life, 20-year-old Jim became a Sunday school teacher at Big Lake Chapel. He expected a large class when he went to the first Sunday school meeting; but only three kids were there. He guessed that there were kids at nearly every farm and home along Big Lake Road and on all the dirt roads branching from it, so during the next week he went door-to-door.

The first house he picked contained two bright-faced girls and a boy. There had been hardship in their family - a divorce, a house fire. They agreed to come. The kids at the next house squirmed shyly but eagerly, and their mother said they could attend.

At one farmhouse door, he met an angry glaring adult face: "Don't come around here trying to get my kids corralled into your churchy world," the man growled.

"Okay," Jim agreed. "How about if they come along for fun? No preaching - just games and singing."

"Yeah, singing. I know your kind of singing. Just don't come back here anymore." The door slammed.

At a cabin pressed between that Finnish farmstead and the next, the Ojibway mother accused

Jim of being just one more in a long line of white missionaries, trying to make her kids believe in a big white God and turn her children into nice little white kids. "And then, when they don't wash pink, you'll kick them in the butt and tell them they're no good. Just leave us alone."

But at the next Indian home, the dad said the kids could go. And kids did come - white and Indian, young and teenaged. Before Jim knew it, he had a large, lively Sunday school class.

*   *   *

Dad decided to build a commercial greenhouse. The LeBorius greenhouse range in Duluth, where he had worked briefly, was being reduced, and some of the glass houses were for sale. Dad dismantled one and brought it home.

Jim, Dad and Dad's brother Walt reassembled it. They scraped tarry caulk from every window and cypress rafter, and gradually the 50-by-25-foot building went up. Jim figured he'd be done in the greenhouse once it was built, but Dad put him to work hammering together tables, hauling dirt, installing a coal-fired furnace. Then they planted seeds - Fireside and Victor tomatoes; cabbage and peppers; petunias and pansies and marigolds. They bought young poinsettias and chrysanthemums and lilies.

And soon the orders for funerals and weddings began coming in. Dad told Jim to handle several wedding arrangements. Mom came in to give him some advice, and to watch. "That's beautiful," she said, after he had completed the third arrangement.

"Well...I don't know how to keep it this way." He shook the vase and the arrangement collapsed. "See? There's some trick to it, but..."

Mom cocked her head, examining the flowers, thinking. "You've got a knack. You ought to go to a school that teaches flower arranging."

So Jim went to Chicago for six weeks, to study at the premiere floriculture school in the nation - Bright School of Floral Design. When he came home, he saw a new sign over the greenhouse: Esala & Son.

One of his first customers was a 17-year-old boy who wanted the "best flower thing" they could make. He was taking his girlfriend to the Junior-Senior Prom at Cloquet High School. "Shirley's got good taste, so you better make it good," the young man said.

"Oh, I'll make it good," Jim said with a smile. "Your lady will love it."

Roger Johnson came back the next day and looked over Jim's creation - a cluster of small orchids and grape hyacinth. He smiled. "What do you call this?"

"A wrist corsage."

"Oh yeah. She's gonna like this, all right." He dug into his pocket and tossed $5 on the counter. "Keep the change."

*   *   *   *   *

Although life in the greenhouse and at Sunday school was rolling along smoothly, life in the Esala home since Gramps moved in was full of tension.

Mealtimes were a torment; Dad and Gramps each pretended the other wasn't there, and conversation withered.

Gramps to Jim: "Pass the salt."

Jim to Dad: "Pass the salt."

Dad gives Jim the salt.

Jim gives the salt to Gramps.

Mom to all: "Pastor Ahlquist will preach on Sunday."

Jim to Dad: "Isn't that the preacher from Mahtowa who bought the Chev?"

Dad to Jim: "Not my Chev."

Mom to all: "I think he is from Mahtowa."

Jim to Gramps: "Was it yours, Gramps?"

Gramps to Jim: "What?"

Jim to Gramps: "The Chev the preacher in Mahtowa bought."

Gramps, former Chev owner, to nobody: "Never had a Chev. Only a bloody fool would buy a Chev."

Dad, current Chev owner, leaps to his feet, slams his chair into place, and leaves the room.

The tension was relieved somewhat by the presence next door of Bud and his family. Bud had married his high-school sweetheart, Jenny, and initially the couple had moved out to the old farm. Now they had two small daughters, and built a home on Esala land, next door to Jim's and Bud's parents. Jim enjoyed having his little nieces so close, and Linda and Colleen skipped in and out of the house on a daily basis.

He took them downtown for ice cream one day, and he ran into his old friend Leo Rabideaux. Leo asked if Jim had heard about a former schoolmate, Dewey Dupuis.

"Just that he's in the Army, an airborne combat team I think."

Some of the county boys were now in Korea, fighting yet another war. Men between the ages of 18 and 35 were being drafted; as World War II veterans, Jim and Bud were exempt. Jim couldn't remember whether Dewey had been drafted or joined up on his own.

"Yeah, army airborne, "Leo said. "Was. He got killed."

"No! How?"

"He was in an attack on some hill over there. They were outnumbered, a whole lot of Chinese held the hill… I dunno, I guess he got shot….He got a stack of medals…."

Medals. Jim remembered a corpse on Corregidor; its disintegrating uniform was decorated with medals. "Lot of good they'll do him," he muttered. He somehow couldn't take it in - that Dewey, with his rakish good looks and buoyant energy, could be turned into a corpse like the dead of Corregidor. He wondered how many others from Cloquet had died. "Have you heard anything about that Roy, the older one - Floyd?"

Floyd Roy, 10 years their senior and a shirttail relative of Leo's (it seemed to Jim like all the Fond du Lac Indians were shirttail relatives) had been serving in Japan when President Truman ordered General MacArthur to commit troops to Korea. Three days after the order, Floyd and the other 405 men comprising Task Force Smith landed, and three days after that they met North Korean/Chinese forces that were pouring into South Korea. In a single day, 150 men from Task Force Smith were killed, wounded or went missing. Floyd hadn't been found.

Leo shook his head. "I was asking Auntie about him just yesterday. Nobody knows anything about him yet - whether he's dead or alive or captured. I'm hoping he just took off and snagged some nice Korean lady, and is in her arms right now."

Long afterwards, they learned that Floyd had been captured and forced on the 120-mile Tiger Death March, named for the murderous North Korean major who commanded it. Another man on the march, an 18-year-old private named Johnnie Johnson, began compiling a secret list of people who perished. The list reached 100 on the march, and another 396 were added later in a prison camp along the Yalu River on the Chinese border. Floyd's name was on it. "Johnson's List" doesn't say the cause of death, but most prisoners at the camp were either executed or died of beatings or starvation. Johnson recorded Floyd's death as July 3, 1951. His remains never were recovered.

Meanwhile, Jim learned that another schoolmate, Billy Kelly, had lost his life when his transport ship went down. The three Cloquet men were among 12 soldiers from the county who perished over a period of 16 months. When Memorial Day rolled around, Jim sent cemetery baskets to Dewey's and Billy's families.

The greenhouse was a busy place; customers bought young tomato plants, petunias for flower boxes, geraniums for Memorial Day baskets. One day a stranger came by. He was about five years older than Jim, and had a confident, happy-go-lucky manner - and a serious limp, which explained why he wasn't in uniform. He was looking for a job, but Dad had none to offer.

"Well, I might as well introduce myself anyhow, because I intend to buy a place around here one of these days," he said to Jim, and stuck out his hand. "Reino Mikkonen."

Reino was from a small town in far northern Minnesota. He could speak a little Finnish. Dad asked him in for dinner.

Gramps, happily, had begun taking his meals in his room upstairs, and a more relaxed atmosphere prevailed.

Elizabeth asked Reino what church he attended.

"I don't."

"How about your folks?"

"They don't either."

Jim cleared his throat. "Then why don't you join us at our church on Sunday?" he asked.

"Thanks, but I don't go to church."

Dad immediately looked suspicious. "You're not a church Finn?"

Reino shot him a wary look. He shook his head.

"Then I guess you must be Red Finn," Dad growled. The rift between "church Finns" and "Red Finns" was as deep in Minnesota as it was back in Finland.

Reino gave him an even look. "I'm an American Finn. Same as you."

"You're not the same as me if you're a god-hating communist Red Finn."

Reino leaned back in his chair and put his hands on his lap. "Well, Mr. Esala, I don't hate anybody, not even your god, and I'm not a communist either, but I've got a right to be one if I want to, same as you got a right to be a holy-roller."

That was too much for Dad; he sat up straight and turned red. "Rights, you talk about! So you are a Red Finn, probably one of those union rabble rousers!"

Reino's face flushed. "I back the unions, if that's what you mean."

"Communist!" Dad leaped to his feet and stomped out the door.

"Maybe I should join the Communist Party, if you're the alternative!" Reino shouted behind him. He turned back to Jim and Elizabeth, appearing a little abashed.

Jim looked at Reino curiously. "You don't believe in God, then?"

"Probably not the way you do."

"What other way is there?"

Reino sighed. "As many ways as there are languages, I bet. But I don't know enough about them to talk about it." He slid his chair back, as though the meal were over.

"There is only one way - the way of Jesus," Jim persisted.

"And just how do you know that?"

"The Word of God - the Bible. It says so."

Reino rose to his feet. "Thank you for that fine meal, Mrs. Esala." he said. He turned to Jim. "There are a lot of word-of-god books in the world, and everybody thinks theirs is the right one." He sent an apologetic look to Elizabeth, took a deep breath, and continued: "A lot of people, including me, think your bible is nothing more than an ancient history book written by a bunch of half-crazy nomads in a faraway desert."

"What!" Elizabeth cried, rising to her feet.

Jim went over to the door and blocked Reino's path. He was curious about this outspoken man, who might after all be an atheist and a communist. He had never met either one before. "So you think some other book does have the Word of God?"

"They're all words of people, as far as I'm concerned."

"Then how can the Lord make Himself known to us?"

"I don't know what you mean by 'the Lord.' What I mean is probably something different." He made another move for the door, but Jim moved too.

"Different?"

Reino thought a moment. "I don't think of 'the Lord,' as you call it, as a person. I think of 'him' as an 'it' - the power behind everything, and we can see that power all around us, in the sky, in the woods, in us, in other animals... I don't have to look very far to find it, if I'm paying attention, and I sure don't find it in a book."

Elizabeth's lips were tight; she was shaking her head.

"That sounds like heathen talk to me," Jim said. "Worshiping creation instead of the God Who made it."

Reino shrugged. "Suit yourself." He turned to Elizabeth. "Thank you again; I have to be going now."

Jim let him through and walked out part way. "So long, then."

"Be seeing you," Reino said with a strained smile, and limped out onto the road to thumb a ride to town.

*   *   *

Jim's mother had suffered ill health all her life, and now it was worse than ever. Dermatitis plagued her. She ached all over. And suddenly, one day, she began hemorrhaging. The diagnosis was uterine cancer. When she tearfully told Walfred what the doctor said, her eyes showing her fear, he just got up and left the room. It was obvious to Jim that after her hysterectomy, her care would be in his hands.

She came through the surgery well, and to help keep her in bed at home as she recovered, Jim got her a *Better Homes and Gardens* subscription. Dad, leafing through it one day to look over the flowers, saw an ad for Watkins. The Minnesota firm had a popular line of spices, linaments and vitamins, and was a big direct-sales company, with more than 200 products and thousands of salesmen in the U.S. and Canada.

Dad became a Watkins man; Elizabeth recovered. Dad's moodiness abated. He threw himself into his new work, traveling around communities to sell the products. He seemed to have a new energy, and he became more mellow, more pleasant, and more concerned for the well-being of others. He was particularly upset when he saw families so poor they couldn't afford clothing for their children.

"Mother, we've got to do something; those kids need clothes," he said to Elizabeth. So he began collecting used clothing from well-to-do people and bringing it back to the greenhouse, where it could be distributed to those who were hard up. Word got around, and soon folks who had extra clothing were bringing in boxes themselves. Many times whole families would come and fit out their children.

But it wasn't long before alcohol sneaked up on him again. He began coming home later and later from his Watkins route. Sometimes he didn't come home at all. The phone at home would ring, a voice from Duluth alerting them that the Watkins truck was stuck in the snow. Jim would have to go fetch the truck before the Watkins liquids froze, and then, if his father wasn't asleep inside, go find him at some wino hangout.

Walfred was in bed sleeping it off one early spring morning, when they were supposed to be starting vegetables in the greenhouse. Jim was tired too, because he had spent part of his night finding his drunken father, but there was much to do in the greenhouse. The morning was cold and the day threatened to stay that way. Jim was adding a little coal to the fire when Reino came in.

"How you doin'?" he greeted Jim.

"OK. How about you?"

"Great!"

Jim could see that his visitor was full of news. He had planned to be cool to Reino - no use pursuing a friendship with someone who scoffs at God. But then he felt guilty; the "Red Finn" was still pretty new in the area, and probably didn't know a lot of people who would listen to his good news.

"What's great?" Jim smiled.

"Well, there are two great things."

"That's even better. What are they?"

"First thing is, I found a good job, over at Diamond Match."

"That is good news."

"Yup." Reino grinned. "And I found a good woman. We got married yesterday."

Jim stopped working and stared at his visitor. This lame communist atheist already had his own life underway, and he'd only lived here a few months? Jim felt a prick of jealousy.

Just then Dad walked into the greenhouse. He was hung over. He glared at Reino.

Reino's good mood kept him from returning the glare. He nodded politely to Walfred, and then said, "Well, I'll be on my way; so long."

After Reino left, Dad turned his glare on Jim. "What did that Red Finn want around here?"

"Just visiting."

Dad snorted. "This is *my* greenhouse. Nobody comes in here I don't want in here. And I don't want him in here."

Suddenly Reino seemed like somebody Jim wanted to come around. "I thought this was *our* greenhouse. Esala *and* Son, you know?"

Dad didn't bother answering. Jim turned back to his work.

Much later in the day, Jim was making a new arrangement of white chrysanthemums, purple lisianthus and purple larkspur. He turned to reach for a wire. And there was Dad, standing right behind him. His eyes were red with anger, and he was holding aloft a pipe wrench as though he were going to hit Jim with it.

Jim suddenly remembered his childhood promise to himself: *Someday, I'm going to be big enough to manhandle my dad.* The time apparently had come. Jim was big, at least four inches taller and more muscular than the older man. He stood facing his father, calm and ready.

Dad was breathing hard. Seconds passed. Then, before Dad even made a move, Jim could feel him retreating. He simply backed down, and no manhandling was necessary.

What had enraged him so? Jim doubted it was Reino. Dad's moods definitely were becoming more erratic. Jim wasn't sure whether the mood swings caused the drinking or vice-versa, but Dad's drinking was out of control.

*   *   *

One Sunday in May, right after church, Jim drove back to the house to get Gramps. The old man, now

89, wanted to see the arrival of the first ocean-going ships in Duluth, a result of the building of the St. Lawrence Seaway. Gramps came slowly down the walk. He was bent over and looked as though he had suddenly become much smaller. He was unusually cheerful, though, and raised his face to the bright morning sun. It was a lovely day in Cloquet.

They drove through town and past Scanlon, and then turned onto Highway 61. Jim could see Gramps, over in the passenger seat, get rigid with fear. The old man's foot worked an imaginary brake. As they neared Duluth, they met cold air from Lake Superior, and Jim raised his window. A little further, and they drove under a cloud bank. By the time they breasted the big hill and began the descent down Cody Street into Duluth, it was raining and windy. Jim turned on the wipers and the heater.

"That's Duluth for you," Gramps muttered. "Bloody town can't maintain a half-decent spring for more than a few hours at a time."

Luckily, there was no fog, and the cloudbank was high enough to allow a misty view of the big lake stretched out to the horizon. The aerial bridge that spanned the two piers of the harbor entrance looked like a miniature erector set creation.

On Superior Street, the traffic was heavy for a Sunday. They turned down Lake Avenue toward the ship canal. Traffic was heavy; it looked like the whole area was turning out for the big day.

Gramps grabbed the door handle and pressed his back hard against the seat.

"Slow down!"

"I'm only doing 15."

"Well it's too fast! And get closer! I can't see nothing from here!"

"I can't get past this line of cars ahead of us. What do you want me to do?"

"Just get there." Gramps' feet were glued to the floor.

The cars finally moved on past Joe Huie's restaurant, past the stripper club and bars and warehouses, until they came to a big open area where people had parked their cars. There was no room to park and they couldn't get any closer to the piers, which were packed solid with people, all the way out to the ends.

There were some sort of formal festivities and someone was making a speech, but they were too far away to hear clearly. But they could see a ship approaching from the lake. As it neared, the crowd began to cheer.

The cheering became deafening as a salt water cargo ship slowly moved between the piers and under the aerial bridge. A few crew members stood in the rain waving at the crowd.

Gramps pulled out his binoculars. "*Ramon de Larrinaga*," he read the inscription on the gold-banded black hull. "I know that name."

"Sounds Spanish."

"She's not. Larrinaga's a British company."

The *Larrinaga* was heading for the Peavey Elevator to take on a load of grain. Colorful flags strung from the mast; the black smokestack had red and gold stripes. Towards the stern were the white-painted living quarters.

Gramps rubbed his grey-whiskered chin; Jim could hear the scratchy noise despite the wind and noise of the crowd. "There's a coincidence here..."

Oh no, here we go, Jim thought. Gramps was always looking for patterns in things, no matter how flimsy they might be; he loved to find parallels. *It must be all those parallel rows in his truck garden that trained his mind that way.*

"This seaway, it's really just a big canal," Gramps continued, "and here, the *Ramon de Larrinaga* comes through right off the bat. Back when the Panama Canal got built, Ramon de Larrinaga came through right away too - not the ship, but the old man himself. Old Ramon was commanding one of the Larrinaga ships."

"How do you know so much about it?"

"I'm an Englishman. We're seafaring people. We know all about ships."

Jim resented Gramps' bluster, and also the way he was always looking for thin connections in things. *He never looks for connections between people, or with the Lord,* Jim thought. *No wonder he's so sour.*

Besides, you could twist anything into a coincidence. How about the twist of fate, you could call it a backwards coincidence, which had him taking Gramps to an entertaining spectacle - this man who never once allowed him and Bud even to leave the farm work to go to the Fourth of July fireworks in Cloquet! Work work work, that's all the old man ever wanted from them. But when he wanted some entertainment, like this, he expected Jim to help him get it.

"She's in ballast," Jim observed, forcing the irritation from his voice.

"What?"

"She's sailing empty, no cargo."

"How would you know?"

Jim's temper flared. "How many ships did you sail, other than the one that brought you to America?" he said scornfully. "If you know so much about ships, being an Englishman, tell me what that water is that's being pumped out the side of this one."

Gramps clamped his mouth shut. He looked furious.

"It's ballast," Jim said. "And it's almost emptied out, which is why she's riding so high in the water. As an Englishman, of course you knew that, and as a sailor, I wouldn't, right?"

Gramps ignored him

The *Larrinaga* passed, and out on the lake another "saltie" from the Atlantic was moving toward the Superior entry. The Liberian-registered *Herald* was on its way to the Globe Elevator.

"We're connected to the world now," Gramps said. "We could sail right out of Duluth all the way to Liverpool or Casablanca." He coughed. "Let's go."

For a second Jim thought Gramps meant, Let's go to Liverpool or Casablanca, and his heart lurched in excitement; in the next second, he had an impulse to leave Gramps where he was, sign onto one of those ships and sail into the Atlantic without a backward look. He felt a little deflated when they had to turn back to Cloquet.

*   *   *

The summer passed, and the greenhouse business was good. One late fall day, Jim left Dad in the greenhouse and went into the house for a cup of coffee. He carried it to the window and sipped it as he watched a car pull into the yard, and a woman with two children enter the greenhouse. A clothing run, he figured. Dad would take care of it.

A moment later the woman came rushing out, looking distraught and calling for help.

Jim dropped his cup and ran into the greenhouse. There he found his father, collapsed in the aisle, unconscious.

The doctor's conclusion was not unexpected. "He's pretty far gone," Dr. Butler said. "He's got bleeding ulcers and his liver is failing. The only chance he's got is if you commit him. He's not well enough to make the decision for himself."

Jim went to court and got the commitment. And then he drove Dad to the old federal prison at Sandstone, 50 miles away, which was being used as a treatment center for alcoholics. When they turned into the lane leading to the center, Dad froze.

"What is this place?"

"A treatment center. So you can get better."

"You're not putting me in here!"

"Dad, you're dying. You have to stop drinking if you're going to stay alive."

"If it wasn't for you I wouldn't drink at all! It's your fault I drink! Turn this car around and take me home!"

Jim pulled up to the door and turned off the engine.

"Let's go, Dad."

"I'll disinherit you! You're no son of mine!" Walfred was too weak to resist, and he was taken into the center.

Jim felt terrible for a long time. His initial visits to the treatment center were difficult; Dad didn't want to talk to him, and it was hard seeing one's father in a prison cell, even one whose doors were unlocked. Eventually, though, Dad adjusted.

During his long drying-out time, he made Jim a leather Bible cover, tooled on the back with his own design: a cross, with a figure clinging to it. Jim felt it was a double treasure - a beautiful cover, and his Dad's forgiveness for having committed him. He still had his own forgiveness to work on, though.

Months later, Dad returned home. He was finished as a Watkins man, but he took a renewed interest in the greenhouse. One day, in the middle of planting a cemetery basket, he went into the house to lie down. He refused to come for supper. Early in the morning, he called Elizabeth: "Mother, I am sick."

In just moments, he lapsed into unconsciousness. Jim called his brother; Bud came right over and called Dr. Butler. But before the doctor arrived, Dad died in Jim's arms.

The next day Jim went out to the greenhouse and puttered there. He looked at the stack of clothing Dad had left on a corner table for the neighbor kids. He looked at the flowers. The place seemed very empty. The anger he had felt toward his father for so long seemed to linger in the building. Jim prayed: "Lord, I don't want any negative feelings in my life. Please help me forgive my father."

He had to finish the cemetery basket Dad had been working on, but it was the hardest job he had ever done.

Shirley

*A*s the only child left at home with aging parents, 15-year-old Shirley turned to a new friend for affection: Roger Johnson, a Cloquet High School student who, at age 17, was already a heavy drinker. Some of her absentee brothers and sisters voiced concern about how his drinking might affect their little sister.

One evening Shirley came home completely drunk, and her dismayed parents asked her brother James to come over and talk some sense into her. James now had his own family and lived in another town, but he came. "I'd never tell anyone else how to live their life; you have to make your own way," he said to his baby sister. "But Shirley, it's important to make sound decisions in your life."

When she was 16, Roger took her to the Junior-Senior Prom, bringing her a lovely wrist corsage he bought at Esala & Son Greenhouse. They got drunk after the prom.

The next year, the couple was married in a Catholic church. They settled in Cloquet, and Roger began a rocky career as a cook. A year later, their only child, Ken, was born.

And then the panic attacks began.

The more a man is united within himself and interiorly simple, the more and higher things doth he understand without labour; because he receiveth the light of understanding from above.

- Thomas á Kempis

CHAPTER 9

Churchianity

It's 2006. I am on my way into Duluth to meet Jim and some of his prayer partners. I pass by a church. It's a newer building, an unattractive concrete sprawl bounded by closely trimmed transplanted hedges that look like a landscape version of mall music. Its parking lot is full, and I see a sign that announces there is some sort of revival going on. There is no activity outside, so the show must already have begun.

As I reach the other side of the building, I notice a man emerging in a hurry from an almost-new Cadillac, which he has parked in a no parking zone by the church. He's white, tall, with wavy gray hair, and is carrying a leather briefcase. He's wearing a grey suit that appears expensive. He's apparently late, but he pauses to smooth his hair carefully and adjust his clothing. He straightens, assumes an authoritative persona, and begins striding purposefully toward the church door.

He must be the main event.

On the rest of my way into town, I think about him: How far has he come? Is he as pretentious as he appears, or is he just trying to do the best he can while battling down butterflies in his stomach? Did he prepare for today's audience with a self-help book - something like *Dressing for Preaching Success*, or *How to Wow the Crowd?* Does he have gas money home? Is he a loving husband, an authoritarian father, a generous friend, a closet gay? Does he really believe whatever it is he's going to preach about?

Then I wonder whether there will be preaching at this meeting I'm going to. And what will they talk about? The rumor that Billy Graham, now 86 and ailing, might go out on another crusade? Islam? The recent death of Pope John Paul II? The papers and magazines have been full of photos surrounding the late Pontiff: his body lying in State; the colorful gathering of cardinals; the streets of Rome flooded with pilgrims and mourners. Maybe they'll talk about Cardinal Ratzinger, the new Pope Benedict XVI...

I arrive at my destination, the Salvation Army building. It's a busy place, half community center and half outreach. Families come here for food shelf, for Christmas gifts, to get emergency housing. Individuals walk in for free lunches; others volunteer their time. It's a friendly, unassuming building, with friendly, unassuming faces inside.

Jim and two of his Christian "brothers" - Gary Wedan and Don Hanson - welcome me and detour me into a little side room. Seated at a table inside is an editor I once worked with. He throws me a big smile that seems to me to be one of relief. I wonder why he's here, and if he was worried I wouldn't show up and he would be stuck alone with these three pious men. They're all good people, not pretentious or judgmental at all, but you know, three preachers together....

We discuss the book. Jim's friends have asked the editor to handle the editing and production end of this project. They talk about that awhile, and the editor says he'll do it, as long as I have the uncensored freedom to write the book as I see it. They have no problem with that; they didn't plan to interfere anyhow.

And then, sure enough, they want to pray. Not only pray, but stand over us - first the stunned-looking editor and then me - and do a "laying on of hands."

I cringe inwardly. I had experienced that only once in my life, 50 years earlier at confirmation, when Bishop Kellogg pressed down on my head so hard I heard my neck creak. It was not a pleasant experience, and I feel tense now. I don't want to offend these kind people by refusing, but neither do I want to be dishonest. I don't really believe the way they do; I believe some of it in a general way, but -

Then it occurs to me that maybe this resistance is just a matter of my own pride. The Proverb, "Pride goeth before destruction, and an haughty spirit before a fall," runs through my mind, a memorized verse which probably was dredged out of the remote past by that confirmation memory. After all, they haven't expected me to believe anything. They've never quizzed me, never demanded that I fall into line with them. They're just offering an open-ended gift. Am I too proud to accept it?

So I accept, and it's not unpleasant at all. Their three hands on my shoulders and head are strong, polite and warm. Their words are heartfelt: "Lord we ask you to guide Susan in her work; stay by her, help her and her family, give her good health." Despite their voices, the room seems strangely quiet, as though not even the air is stirring. I feel surrounded by a glow of genuine affection.

We then adjourn to a larger room, where the "Wednesday Night Group" is gathering. About a dozen men, many of them in early middle age, meet here weekly to discuss spiritual matters and everyday problems, and to pray together. Much-used Bibles are taken out of briefcases and protective coverings and opened on the table. Talk is wide-ranging and personal. Most of the men are well mannered and seem to be educated. I sit way off to one side, taking notes for this book. I'm the only woman here. Nobody seems to mind my presence, either as a woman or as a nonparticipating observer.

One man tells about a young white evangelist who was passing out tracts in a poor African-American neighborhood. At one apartment, a young woman holding a baby and smoking a cigarette gave him a guarded look. Looking past her through the open door, he could see two other young children, one still in diapers, playing on the floor, and an apartment showing serious poverty - not much furniture, open and nearly empty kitchen cupboards. He tried to pass her a tract as he talked about salvation, and she told him to leave her alone and slammed the door. As he walked away, he thought about what had happened. This woman was actually in a desperate situation; she needed material help, not a tract. So he went shopping and returned to the home with a box of groceries, a carton of cigarettes and a big package of disposable diapers. This time she smiled in relief and tearfully asked him in.

There are murmurs of approval around the table:

"That's being a servant of God."

"We need to minister to each other like that."

"We can't judge people; we are supposed to help them."

One of the men wonders how a person can do that: become aware of the needs of others, then feel the need to help them, and then follow through with the help.

"Remember - the veil was torn," Don says.

It's evident others are as puzzled as I am by this seemingly free-floating statement.

"The temple veil separated ordinary people from the Holy of Holies, which was the seat of God, ever since the time of Moses," Don explains. "The high priest could go behind the veil once a year, on behalf of the people, to atone for their sins; but no one else could go back there. In other words, ordinary people were separated from God; they needed priestly intercession to have a connection with Him.

"But Jesus changed that. When He died, and darkness descended on the land and the earth quaked and rocks fell apart, the temple veil was rent in twain from the top to the bottom."

More puzzled expressions.

"Now each and every one of us can come into the presence of God and ask forgiveness for our sins. There is no veil between us and the Lord. We need no priests or preachers. We can draw close to Him, and in that intimacy we are given the guidance, the awareness and the ability to reach out to others in love - like that young evangelist with the groceries."

I feel touched by this clear, unassuming yet profound interpretation of a biblical event of which I had somehow remained ignorant through all those Easter Week services I had to attend as a child. Others seem similarly touched.

But one man seems to have got stuck on the words "high priest," for he begins talking about Catholics. Another joins him in what becomes a surprisingly savage attack. The two move on to Pope John Paul II, then to his successor. We are told with glowering expressions that the new pope used to be a Nazi and that he remains the personification of evil.

"If you look at his photographs very carefully, you can see horns on his head," the second man confides knowingly.

Horns? I suddenly feel sick. Images race through my mind: Crusaders and Cossacks slaughtering "horned" Jews; Puritans slaughtering "horned" Indians. Apparently that old Devil visual to unify barbaric Christians is still around. Put Satan's horns on somebody in your imagination, and you can regard him as non-human. Then it's okay to kill him, since Christians don't seem to think obliterating non-humans is a sin.

Once again the thought emerges: *Maybe I shouldn't be doing this book.* I gauge how far it is to the door; can I leave without attracting too much attention?

But then I look at Jim again, and he has the tolerant expression he gets when he is in the presence of what he calls "immature believers" - people who still need to learn the greatest commandment. Don and most of the others have similar expressions. Nobody picks up on the subject, and it dies for lack of interest. The talk returns to love.

All through the meeting, Jim has said very little. He listens thoroughly to each man's remarks, and only occasionally inserts his own quiet comment.

Later, I ask him about his role in the group. From what some of his prayer partners had told me earlier, I thought that he was the leader, but he didn't act like one.

"No, no, I'm not the leader," he says. "I wouldn't want to be. The Lord is the only leader we need."

Then I tell him about the man I saw on my way here - the hired preacher who was walking across the parking lot. I describe him closely, particularly his appearance of self-importance.

"You see that a lot," Jim says. "I can't judge what's in his heart, of course, but whenever you put yourself out there as an expert, and people treat you that way and especially if they give you money for it, there's a problem. You start thinking you're special, and so do others. Then you stray from the path. The way to God is not through the admiration of others, and it's not through a man or an organization."

*   *   *

But we humans do like to organize ourselves, even in matters of faith. How much? The next day, I decide to check.

There are about 6 billion believers among the Earth's 6.5 billion people, I read. They are roughly distributed among the following religious beliefs:

Christianity - 2 billion
Islam - 1.5 billion
Hinduism - 1 billion
Chinese traditional religion (including Taoism
    and Confucianism) - 400 million
Buddhism - 380 million
Indigenous (in the Americas, Siberia, Africa) -
    320 million
African-based (including Santeria and Voudoun)
    - 115 million
Sikhism - 23 million
North Korean Juche - 18 million
Judaism - 15 million
Spiritism - 15 million
Baha'i - 7 million
Jainism - 4 million
Shintoism - 4 million

Cao Dai (Vietnam) - 4 million
Unitarian Universalist - 1 million
Other (Rastafarianism, Zoroastrianism,
    Scientology, Tenriko, Wikka, Druidism, etc.)
    - 6 million

Many of these religions are further subdivided, into often argumentative and sometimes violently antagonistic denominations. Islam has Sunnis, Shi'ites, Sufis. Judaism has Orthodox, Conservative, Reform. Hinduism has Vaishnavaism, Shivaism, Smartism. Buddhism has Theravada, Mahayana, Zen.
Christians, of course, are divided too:

Roman Catholic - 1.1 billion
Protestant - 450 million
Orthodox (Russian, Ethiopian, Assyrian, Greek,
    Serbian, Coptic etc.) - 240 million
African indigenous sects - 110 million
Anglican/Episcopalian- 73 million
Jehovah's Witness - 15 million
Latter-Day Saints (Mormons) - 13 million
Seventh-Day Adventist - 12 million
New Thought (including Christian Science and
    Unity) - 1.5 million
Friends (Quakers) - 300,000

Among the Protestant Christians alone are:

Pentecostal - 110 million
Reformed/Congregational/United/Presbyterian
    - 75 million

Baptist - 70 million
Methodist - 70 million
Lutheran - 65 million
Apostolic/New Apostolic - 10 million
Restoration Movement (Stone-Campbell) -
    5 million
Brethren - 1.5 million
Mennonite - 1.2 million...
and others.

And even these are subdivided into groups that would prefer not to worship together. Oneness Pentecostals and Trinitarian Pentecostals. Wisconsin Synod Lutherans, Missouri Synod Lutherans and ELCA Lutherans. Southern Baptists and American Baptists.

"All these divisions!" Jim exclaims. "It starts with little irritations, wedges and dissension. We even get it at the men's group. And we can't afford to have dissension. Loving one another, praying for one another, that's how we close the gap.

"These denominations all say they're following the same Lord - the One Who wants us to love one another, to come together in prayer and fellowship. That's what matters - not all this 'churchianity.'"

"Churchianity? What's that?" I ask, although I can guess.

Jim elaborates: Churchianity places a denomination or a man or even a building at its center. But, being of human invention, it must develop rules and a social system; and a rule-ridden hierarchy isn't easily reconciled with the simple teachings of the poor carpenter from Nazareth. It has to spend too much energy and attention on keeping its own bureaucracy going. The minister's ego often grows to an unspiritual size. Meanwhile, Jesus slips out the door.

"I'm not anti-church and I'm not judgmental, but we have a lot of churchianity out there," Jim says. "People get comfortable in their little groups; they memorize the Word and support the work, but there's not much fruit in their lives. Instead, they stay comfortable in the pews - while the work of the ministry is outside the door, in the marketplace.

"There are a lot of rules, a lot of regimented stuff, in the denominations. I love the people in them; they're lovely people, they're like my family. But there is a lot of man-made doctrine."

I think of an article I just read in the magazine *Crisis,* which drove home to me the distinctly unspiritual side to man-made doctrine. It was about the "mega-church" phenomenon - Christian churches with up to 40,000 members who gather en masse in flamboyant arena-sized naves and pray mightily for personal prosperity. In the lengthy article, theologians debated the value of such churches; but there was not a single reference to Jesus, salvation, the Cross, Christ's teachings, love or even Christianity. Instead, the discussion was which way churches should lean: toward a liberation theology of social justice; or toward the mega-church model led by "entrepreneurial ecclesiastical executives" who promise individual wealth and group political power.

That's "churchianity" gone amok, in Jim's view. In our pride and greed, he says, we strive to circumvent in every way possible what Jim sees as the simple, unchanging and eternal guidelines of the Almighty. We build elaborate structures of self-serving dogma - the "regimented stuff" which Jim sidesteps as deftly as he sidesteps whatever the day's sensational news might bring.

An example of this disregard of dogma is Jim's attitude toward the ordination of women. Rather than perusing scripture in order to develop an ideology about the matter, Jim just takes it one day at a time, as it comes. On one of those days, Jim and several of his male prayer partners went into Duluth to listen to a "prophet" who had been in the ministry for 30 years and was said to be an anointed person. Jim describes the event: how God had used the pastor, how powerful the meeting was, and how spiritually uplifted he felt later.

"She really ministered to us," he concludes.

"She?" I ask in surprise. "The pastor is a woman?"

"Yes. ...She was here once before, several years back. I was really glad I went again this time. She had a good message - that we need to be close to God and have that intimacy. And she had a word for different individuals, and for me. It was an encouragement, at a time when I needed encouragement."

I pass right over his comment about needing encouragement, hard-headedly homing in on the issue of gender.

"I thought conservative Christians don't approve of women pastors," I snap.

"Don't they? Well, I try to be open. God is using Becky; I can't stand against that."

*   *   *

Later the next day, I give Jim a call. I ask him an easy question first - easy for me, because his answer isn't likely to require changes in the book, which is already half done.

"What do you think of Billy Graham?"

He thinks a moment. "I have a lot of respect for him," he finally says. He explains how as a young man he made a trip down to the Twin Cities to see the evangelist - and to hear the singing of George Beverly Shea, whose 96-year-old voice years continues to move him today.

"Billy Graham has never changed his message, through all these years: You've got to come to the cross. Jesus resurrected. He's *alive*. His resurrected life gives us the freedom from sin.

"That's quite a message, and Billy Graham stays right on it even though he reaches out to people of every faith and nationality. He got a call to preach in his life and he was obedient. He isn't perfect, but he's obedient. And there never have been any questions about his integrity or his morals, the way there have been with some of these other popular evangelists."

Then for the more difficult question - difficult for me, because Jim's answer could fundamentally change the book. I'm nervous; I confuse my syntax and make a statement, instead of posing a question:

"The other night...about Roman Catholics - a couple of the men, they were pretty hard on them," I say. "I've never asked you what you think about it, about Catholicism; or Pope John Paul II."

Jim ignores the garbled sentence structure; his natural inclination is to go for the intention, rather than to dwell on exact wording.

He pauses to collect his thoughts. "Well, I tell you," he says. "I hope he's with the Lord now. He stood for Life and he fought communism, and I appreciate that about him.

"But when a billion people have faith in an organization that is headed by one human being, there's a problem. What if all that mass of people would lift up Jesus the way they lift up the Pope? Wouldn't that be something? The same goes for Protestants - Evangelicals, Pentecostals. Jesus said, 'I am the truth and the life. No man comes to the Father except through me.' You have to be obedient, and not get caught up in the mechanics of running an organization.

"We are the ambassadors. We ARE the church. We represent Him on Planet Earth."

If we don't stand up for children, then we don't stand for much.

- Marian Wright Edelman

CHAPTER 10

Grizz

In the years following the death of his father, Jim found himself increasingly surrounded by kids. They flocked to him: some like playful, colorful finches to a birdfeeder; others, more like bedraggled abandoned nestlings looking for refuge. They came for Jim's dependable, cheerful ways, and also for his mother's affection, cakes and cookies. They called Jim "Essie" - short for Esala - and "Grizz," because he was as big and hairy as a grizzly.

At first, children entered his life through the Big Lake Chapel's Sunday school, for which he was both chauffeur and teacher. Gradually, activities and events outside the Sunday school grew - helping kids in trouble; bringing youngsters to prayer meetings in other communities; getting cones all around at Bridgeman's ice cream parlor.

The ice cream trips brought Reino Mikkonen into the greenhouse. He was wearing a broad, teasing smile.

"I hear you're manipulating children into your religious ways, Jim!"

"How are you doing, Reino?" He reached out for a handshake. "What's all this about manipulating?"

"Ice cream. You've been bribing the younger set with ice cream, so I hear."

Jim smiled. "Bribing, eh? I never thought of it that way. Don't you ever buy ice cream?"

"Sure, but I'm not the one griping about all the cones you're buying. It's some of your so-called Christian brethren - those fellas with the turned-around collars who spout the Word of God all day. A bunch of them were having coffee at Rudy's on Thursday, and they were talking about you. Gossiping, more like. How you run around preaching and don't even have a permit - is that like a dog license? And how you bribe these teenagers to go to your church. They made you look like some kind of Pied Piper piping their young'uns off to perdition."

Jim laughed. He knew that religious teachings weren't what drew most of the kids. Some of the girls came along because they had a crush on him. When the kids piled into his 1957 Ford Sedan delivery truck (and they sometimes packed in an amazing 15, in layers), several girls always fought to sit next to him, and he often had to readjust the seating arrangement to divert their youthful ardor. Some of the boys came solely because they yearned for adult male leadership. And all of them, including himself, enjoyed the ice cream.

"What's your favorite flavor?"

"Oh no, you don't," Reino exclaimed, stepping back in mock alarm. "Don't try to catch me with your ice cream wiles!"

Jim smiled. "Well, it's no concern of mine what those pastors think, and I'm not even pushing too hard on the kids to find the Lord. I'm just concerned to do what seems right to do. Jesus will take care of the rest. If the only reason we went on a ride was to get ice cream, that would be a good enough reason for me."

*   *   *

One of the youngsters who would become one of "Jim's kids" entered his life on a cigarette run for a heavy-equipment operator working a highway job in front of the Esala home. Seven-year-old Donnie strode into the greenhouse and looked around purposefully.

"Where did you come from?" Jim asked, looking down at the small, barefooted Ojibway boy.

Donnie looked up at the big man holding the flowers. He held out the money the operator had given him, and gestured toward the construction project. "That guy out there wants some cigarettes."

"Sorry, we don't sell them." Jim said in a friendly way.

Donnie looked around the greenhouse. It was a little messy. "I'm looking for a job," he said. "Do you want me to clean up here?"

Jim laughed. "Sure! You can start today. Go tell that fellow out there that you found new employment."

And so began a father-son friendship that remains lively today:

> *Jim Esala is the best friend I ever had and the only father I ever knew. Today, I look back and thank the Creator for him. He treated me just like a son. When I was a little kid, I was like a woodtick: Wherever he went, I went. I could depend on him, I could trust him - and I still can. I never met a better man in my life.*

On that first day, Donnie went into the Esala house to use the bathroom. He came running back with a frightened look on his face.

"What's wrong?" Jim asked.

"There's a witch in there!" Donnie gasped.

"A witch? How do you know?"

"I saw her! She asked me if I wanted some cookies or cake! That's how she caught Hansel and Gretel!"

Jim laughed, took him by his hand, and brought him into the house to introduce him to his mother, who gave him a piece of cake. After that, Donnie was completely at home in the Esala house. He could come any time of the day or night, played with Jim's nieces like sisters, and became one of the family.

Gradually Jim realized that more was happening outside of Sunday school than in it. Not only the children, but he himself was growing weary of the rote lessons, the dry curriculum that must be followed. In fact, he was becoming disenchanted in general with the rules and regulations of the formal church organization.

Almost unaware, Jim was moving into the "marketplace" - relating to children, and to others, just as they were, and just as he was. He began doing outreach, visiting troubled adults and troubled families, and helping or praying with them. Donnie usually came along, and often other youngsters did too. Many times, kids would go with him to lend their singing voices at some mission in Duluth, rowdily singing gospel songs on the way.

Sisters Andrea and Sharon were among the girls who had a crush on Jim. "All the girls adored him, and the boys respected him," Sharon said recently. "After awhile, he had so many kids who wanted to be with him, he had to buy a bus to take us all around in."

They liked being with him partly because he loved to have fun, although some might consider his idea of fun a little extreme. Like the Halloween Jim took a bunch of kids up to the Ditchbank home of the one-legged bachelor everyone called "Pegleg Tom." Jim told them that Pegleg had died and the house now was abandoned - it certainly looked that way - and that it was haunted. He dared them to go across the field, walk all through the house, and then come back again. When they got inside, they heard the pegleg - clunk, clunk - coming down the stairs. Howling in terror, they raced back to Jim, who was bent over with laughter. "I must have heard wrong," he guffawed. "Pegleg must still live there!"

On another Halloween, some of the kids begged for some excitement, like a haunted house. So Jim took a truckload of them to a little rustic cabin he and his brother had on Big Lake. It was late at night.

"I'll give anybody five bucks who can bring my old Navy picture out of the cabin, and another five bucks if you bring my brother's," Jim said. "You can't use any light - no matches, no flash. You have to do it all in the dark."

Donnie, niece Linda and a boy named Denny said they'd go; Donnie and Linda knew exactly where the photos were. But inside, feeling their way around the room and whispering together, they became aware of a presence. Breathing. A form.

"Hey, somebody's sitting in this chair!" Donnie exclaimed softly.

"Where?" Linda asked.

"It's OK," Denny said aloud. "It's just a dummy."

Donnie kicked it. It kicked him back.

He yelled, the other kids shrieked, and - since Jim had locked the front door behind them - they scrambled for a window, threw it open and dove out.

They found Jim and the other kids doubled over with laughter. Jim had arranged with a neighbor to sit in the chair, and had a CB radio set up between the cabin and the van, so they could listen to the trio's conversation.

On several other nighttime occasions, he took kids out to the fire tower deep in the woods at the Cloquet Forestry Center, and offered money to anyone who made it to the top of the structure - in the dark.

"Can you believe it, an adult taking kids up a forestry tower in the black of night?" niece Colleen exclaimed. "Nowadays, they would lock him up! Oh, he was so much fun! We all had so much fun!"

*   *   *

A neighbor complained to Jim about teenagers who were speeding past their homes along Big Lake Road. "Aw, they don't mean any harm," he told her. "You know how kids are: They like to lay a patch of rubber and then measure it."

But she was adamant, so Jim stopped a couple of the older boys one day.

"Why don't you tear up the back forty instead of laying rubber on the highway?" he suggested, gesturing toward Esala land behind the house. "Build yourselves a racetrack back there."

They eagerly fell to, and soon they had a race-track that became a teenage gathering place. They raced cars, sometimes hitting the trees; they showed off and flirted with one another; everyone had a lot of fun. The rules were simple: Don't drive into the deer yard (Jim had fenced in a big area for deer, and fed them there); don't tear up the lawn.

Jim came out one evening while Pete, one of the boys who used the strip, was leaving. Sure enough, the lawn was torn up, and Jim scolded him. Not long afterward, Pete was sent to Vietnam. Jim thought about him in the faraway jungle, as the death toll rose and the news came back about the suffering there. He walked back to look at Pete's tire marks. *Here, Pete's gone now; what did I get on his case for?* he asked himself regretfully. *Maybe he'll be hurt over there, maybe he won't even come back....*

He said a prayer for Pete.

Another of "Jim's kids" was Steve, whom Jim first encountered when he got a call from the Cloquet hospital that a young couple and a newborn baby needed a ride home. Reservation roads were rutted and muddy with the spring thaw, and after a bumpy ride home, Jim's car couldn't make it the last half mile to the house. So they walked - the father helping the mother, and Jim carrying baby Steve.

"Little did Jim know that he would be forming a bond that would last the next 48 years," Steve said recently. "Sometimes I think he's still carrying me."

Two incidents bracket Steve's view of Jim: One showing the older man's understanding, and the other his unbending adherence to his view of what is right. When Steve was about 15, he was walking into Cloquet to see - he hoped - a certain girl. As usual, he didn't have a penny, and he was a little nervous about how he was going to approach this girl. Passing the greenhouse, he stopped in to visit. When Jim learned he wanted to impress a girl, he selected a lovely long-stemmed rose, wrapped it carefully and presented it to Steve. "Give this to her like a gentleman; she's sure to like it." She did, too.

The other incident was about five years later. Steve had been attending Jim's storefront mission in Cloquet, and there he met and fell in love with a young woman who occasionally came to the mission. They decided to get married, but couldn't agree on the venue. She wanted a Catholic church;

Steve didn't want a church at all. They decided to compromise with their friend Jim. The pair came to the greenhouse, hand-in-hand.

"We're getting married next week, Jim, and we want you to do the ceremony," Steve announced.

Jim looked at the young couple. He said nothing.

"Well?" Steve said. "How about it?"

"Next week, you say?"

"Yup."

"Are you really ready for such a big step?"

"Sure! The sooner the better!"

He thought awhile. "I can't do that, kids," he finally replied.

They looked surprised and deflated.

"What? Why not?"

"Let me ask you a question before I answer that one. How many happy marriages do you know?"

They hemmed and hawed and came up with a determined statement that they would be different.

"You think so now," Jim said. "But marriage is a lifelong proposition. It takes commitment and love and respect. And those things are hard to come up with, if you don't make God the center of your life. You've seen the same families I've seen - the drunkenness, husbands beating their wives, wives neglecting their children - "

"Oh, we'd never do that!" Steve exclaimed.

"Those couples didn't think so either. They all started out just like you, feeling sure their marriages would be perfect."

The couple was silent.

"If I'm going to do your marriage," Jim continued. "I'll want to counsel with you for an extended period. I'll want to pray with you, help you get a firm foundation - the Lord's. It's easy to love one another when there aren't any problems. But real love is having respect and being patient with one another when you do have problems, and knowing how to talk out your differences so they don't get out of hand."

Steve and his fiancée felt a little glum as they left. They decided against all that pre-nuptial fuss and just went out and got married. And as Jim predicted, it didn't work out.

Steve recently described Jim's stand then as "the most respectful thing I ever saw. He didn't bend one inch when it came to two young kids about to make the biggest mistake of their lives. In all these years, I have never seen him waver from his high moral standards."

*   *   *

Kenny came into Jim's life on his mother Shirley's coattails. The little boy would call sobbing, worried about his mother, wondering if she were dead someplace. Sometimes he needed food, sometimes reassurance, sometimes a place to sleep. One unusually snowy winter, when blizzard followed blizzard, Kenny moved in. He helped in the greenhouse, tried to attend to his ninth-grade schoolwork, and looked forward to spring and football, for which he had a special talent.

It turned out he had a talent for business as well, and Jim put him to handling change and waiting on customers. Kenny got a little impatient with Jim's habit of opening the till and handing out "loans" to anyone who asked.

"What are you doing that for?" Kenny asked him. "There was only $30 in the till, we needed it to pay for those plants that are coming in, and you just gave $20 to a drunk who's going to spend it on wine and never pay you back!"

"Jack said he needed it," Jim said. "That's good enough for me."

Ken lived with the Esalas for a year, and then moved back home. Several years later, he landed a college football scholarship. During his second year, a scout for the Minnesota Vikings, on the lookout for a young quarterback who could follow an aging Fran Tarkenton, wanted to draft him for Vikings' spring training in the southern Minnesota town of Mankato. It was Ken's first big chance in his rocky life - a dream come true - and he could hardly comprehend his good fortune.

"Can you believe it?" he asked Jim excitedly. "The Vikings!" His radiant grin seemed to fill the greenhouse. "I can't even...I mean - I *love* football! Now it looks like I could even get paid to play!"

Jim grinned. "What do your folks think?"

"I haven't told them; I haven't found them yet."

A few days later, Ken stopped in again. The exuberance was gone, replaced by a look that was part bitterness and part sad resignation.

"What's up?" Jim asked. He hoped the draft chance hadn't dried up. What a cruelty that would be.

"Nothin' much." After a long silence, Ken added off-handedly, "I'm not going to Mankato." Slowly he explained: He had finally found his mother. He told her the good news. Instead of being happy for him, she begged him not to go, and ultimately elicited a promise from him to stay home - to skip his dream.

"Why?"

"She said she'd have a nervous breakdown if I left." Ken kicked at a discarded Oriental lily lying on the floor. "She probably would, too."

Jim knew that likely was true. Shirley, who was still drinking, had devastatingly severe panic attacks which sometimes put her in the hospital. She was a genuinely needy person, and for the past decade Ken had been one of her primary supports.

Jim sighed and put a hand on Ken's shoulder. "Something like that happened to me when I was about your age," he said. "It's hard. But if the decision feels right to you, it probably is right, no matter how much it hurts."

Ken nodded. "I know it's right. I mean, she's my mom." Then his voice broke. "But Jim, *football!*"

*   *   *

Not all parents were pleased with their kids' affection for Jim Esala. One father locked up his kids to prevent them going to church with Jim; they climbed out the window.

Another father - a Swede whom Jim was trying to convince to quit beating his children - yelled, "You black Finlander, you mind your own business! These are *my* kids and I'll raise them the way I want to!"

The mother of another boy, an eight-year-old named Francis, ordered Jim to leave her son alone. She complained that the boy was singing gospel songs around the house; he was talking like a holy roller, and they were Catholic.

"I don't search Frankie out, Darlene," Jim said. "He comes over here on his own." He didn't mention that the boy arrived hungry, dirty and half dressed. Jim's mother had been giving him baths and meals, and fitting him out with clothing.

Darlene returned a couple of weeks later. She had been drinking. "You damn *chimokes*, always grabbing, grabbing! You got our Indian land, now you want our kids? Frankie's *my* son!"

"Then treat him like he's yours," Jim said. "Take better care of him; he needs you. He's just a little boy, and he's out all hours and he's hungry. The other day, I saw a couple of bruises on his back; how'd he get those? Who's hitting him?"

Before he could duck, Darlene backhanded him so hard it split the skin on his jaw. Then she hit him on the other jaw, and stalked off.

Frankie was persistent despite his mother's objections; he kept visiting the Esalas and became firmly one of "Jim's kids." But the boy also looked out for his mother. He kept dropping hints about how she and his two little brothers needed help. So Jim began accompanying him home, to fix the pump (the family had no running water), replace broken window panes, split wood. Elizabeth sent the family cakes and hot dishes.

The years passed. When casino revenues brought new jobs and better housing, Darlene was able to get employment and move her family into a house with running water and gas heat. Frankie grew up and moved away.

One day, Jim received an invitation to Darlene's retirement party. It was an elaborate event, with a special table for those being honored. Jim was ushered to the front and seated with Darlene and her family. She introduced him to the dignitaries as her special guest.

During the speeches, she turned to him. "*Migwetch*, Jim," she murmured. "Thanks for being a friend, a *real* friend, all these years."

*　　*　　*

Recently, some of "Jim's kids" reminisced about him:

"I was scared of most of the adult figures around me. But Jim was so tolerant. He was a truly decent man; I felt I could put my life in his hands." - *Cookie*.

"Every day is a new start for Jim, a new adventure. Even if he has to do the same old monotonous thing, he does it with care and kindness, ever thoughtful of others' feelings. He would have made a great father. In some ways, he's been like a father to me." - *Steve*.

"He was never too busy to lend an ear. He was always there for us, no matter what we did, no matter how bad we were, and he never gave up on any of us. Never had there been anyone in our lifetime with as much patience as he had for each of us through our growing-up years. If we were troubled or had family problems, which most of us did from time to time, he would be there to rescue us. We all loved him so much." - *Sharon*.

"I have a very good life now, and without Grizz, it might not have happened. I had wonderful experiences because of him and with him - I got a belief in God through him. That man will do anything for anyone; he helped many, many people, including my mother. You don't forget something like that." - *Francis*.

"He was so patient with us, so kind. He never lost his temper with us, ever, not even when we were mischievous or acting bad." - *Andrea*.

"Jim is a rock, the kind of guy people can depend on. Just to know that he is available to be phoned at a moment's notice, 24/7, often provides struggling people like my mom - and for me today, to be candid - the confidence that somebody cares. And he never, never gives up." - *Ken*.

Some people want to know how to start a mission:
Well, it starts in your heart. Otherwise, it's nothing.
A mission is a door that's always open, and never
closes. It's a heart experience.

- Jim Esala

CHAPTER 11

Missions

It is a sunny morning in mid-May. Jim is taking me to see the various locations where he and his prayer partners established missions.

"The word 'mission' has always impressed me," he says, as he makes a turn at an odd-shaped structure said to be the only gas station ever designed by the famed architect Frank Lloyd Wright. Like other local people, he drives past it without a glance or comment.

"The dictionary has several definitions," he continues. "The one I like is, 'a special task to which one devotes one's calling.' That describes my mother's and grandmother's lives. And they were the ones who taught me - so my whole life became a mission."

We leave Cloquet and enter the little village of Scanlon. Jim pulls up at a mostly abandoned light industrial site, and points to a small collapsed structure surrounded by last year's tall brown weeds. The new leaves on some young birch and popple frame it in a cloud of green lace.

"A fella named Carl lived here," Jim says. "He developed a bad drinking problem, lost his job at the mill, and this became a wino hangout. Finns from Esko, tramps from the railroad, Indians from the rez - men and women, they came here to Carl's to drink. My dad hung out here too, before he died."

He falls into a silent reverie for a moment, then adds, "This became our first mission building."

"How did that happen?"

"Well, I used to pick up Carl sometimes, bring him home for a meal, and I saw how his home was deteriorating. It got really bad, with all the winos hanging out there. Went from a nice little home to a really filthy place, no lights, no heat, no running water; they used the closet for a toilet, and when that got filled they started in on the bathtub. I mean filthy."

And then one day, down in the Cloquet public sauna, Jim was telling Donnie and a new prayer partner, Joel Kulaszewicz, about Carl's place. Joel was a local meter reader and was familiar with the dramatic deterioration of Carl's once lovely little home. They decided to clean it up, if Carl was willing.

"Carl was happy about it," Jim says. "So I borrowed my brother's truck and we hauled out filthy furniture and garbage, and got the place halfway livable. Then we asked Carl if he would like to have some prayer meetings there. 'Oh, that would be wonderful!' he said. We brought over some old 78s and an old record player, and started having meetings there."

Carl was still drinking, and it was still a wino hangout, but it had become a mission. The winos didn't seem to mind the missionaries, perhaps because the latter never told them they would go to hell if they kept drinking.

"They already knew that," Jim says. "What they needed was to have someone say to them, 'Hey, we care about you,' and we did."

"You did what - you mean you told them?" I ask, a little suspiciously.

"We did care," Jim responds gently.

One of the drinkers had been a prosperous businessman in Cloquet, but his drinking cost him everything - wife, kids, business. Jim's group prayed with him and then took him to Lake Venoah, a nearby treatment center, and he was completely rehabilitated.

"That's when I learned that you don't try to bring the drunks to church; what church in town would welcome a drunk? You go where the drunks are," he said.

A couple of preachers in town asked him where he was finding all these alcoholics; there weren't really that many in Cloquet, were there? Jim realized that they didn't have any idea how serious the problem was, and they didn't know about it because they didn't look. They didn't see the problem of alcohol, and they didn't see the problem of poverty either.

"We started going out into the neighborhoods, and found poverty plus," Jim said. "We brought people food. We went down to the teenagers' keg parties in the woods and talked to them, trying to keep them out of trouble; the parents wouldn't do it, so we did. One of the teen girls came to Sunday school crying because her dad had whipped her with willow switches and locked her in the basement, and I had to go talk to him."

The church board got wind of their Sunday-school teacher's extracurricular activities and called him to account. They sat in a circle around him, very politely, but Jim felt like he was going to the slaughter.

"You're getting too involved in domestic affairs," one of the men announced, and the others nodded. "You're interfering in personal lives in the community."

"Isn't that what it's all about - involvement in personal lives?"

"But you're not a pastor. You don't have the training. We want you to back off, and we'll take care of these matters."

Jim took a deep breath and stood up. "We're all pastors for one another, and I'm not going to stop being involved with people," he said. "The disciples didn't go to divinity school, and the apostle Paul didn't get a certificate or a license to practice..."

He thought a moment, and then began walking toward the door. "And they didn't have a board of directors telling them what to do, either," he added over his shoulder. "So I think I'll just follow their lead."

He bid them and organized religion goodbye, and became an independent missionary - to drunks, to kids, and to whomever he felt directed.

*   *   *

But he was having financial problems. Although the greenhouse had been bringing in enough income for ordinary living expenses, extraordinary bills were piling up. Bills from his father's funeral and his mother's cancer surgery were still largely unpaid; and Jim's regular partial payments weren't making enough headway to stall off collections. In addition, Gramps had died and that funeral bill was outstanding; and Mom had recently been hospitalized again. In today's dollars, it all added up to more than $30,000. He fretted; he broke out in cold sweats. *I can't leave a sinking ship,* he thought. *What am I going to do?*

One morning he took all the bills, put them in an envelope, and went to see a bankruptcy attorney. But as he watched the lawyer go through the paperwork and start taking notes, he suddenly stood up.

"I changed my mind," he said abruptly, and picked up the bills and left. He went straight to the collection agency for St. Luke's Hospital. The short, stout older man handling the account was friendly and accommodating. "We can work this out," he assured Jim.

A friend who worked at Minntac, a taconite processing company on Minnesota's Iron Range, found Jim a job as a carpenter. He had to close the greenhouse, but he could come home every night, and the money - union scale - was good. Once a month, the hospital collection agent came to the Esala home and picked up a check. The two men would have coffee together. Jim actually looked forward to these monthly visits, and when eventually the bill was paid off, he felt a little sorry

Mission work continued - both at home and up on the Iron Range. At Minntac, and later on other construction jobs, Jim's "clean" life - no swearing, no stealing of tools, no criticism of others, no drinking or chasing women - eventually attracted the attention of his co-workers. Some of those who were the most scornful of him in public would seek him out in private to confide their troubles, and ask him about God or salvation. Prayer meetings during lunch periods and after work were established. Jim was finding construction work to be a font of friendship and spiritual growth.

The mission at Carl's house was moved to an upstairs apartment on Dunlap Island, where long ago Jim had delivered vegetables with his grandfather. That place was even livelier than Carl's, and the group soon outgrew it. They moved to another building before settling in a storefront in Cloquet's old downtown - at 120 Avenue C. "Faith Rescue Mission," they called it, and put a neon cross on the front.

It was at this time that Jim had the greatest experience of his life: what charismatic Christians call the "baptism of the Holy Ghost." That's when the Holy Spirit fills the believer, and gives him or her one or more gifts - *healing, speaking in tongues, inter-*

pretation, wisdom, knowledge, faith, discernment, prophesy, miracle-working. He or she also receives the nine fruits of the spirit that are the outward and visible signs of an inward and spiritual grace: *love, joy, peace, longsuffering, gentleness, goodness, faith, meekness* and *temperance.*

This life-changing experience came about as a result of the visit of some Filipino missionaries - Brother Roberto, and Sisters Pasida, Evelyn and Raphina. They were traveling with an American missionary, Brother Shields, and began having revivals in Duluth.

Jim attended one, and felt uncomfortable. People were clapping, stamping their feet, raising their arms, dancing, and speaking in tongues. Several people fell over like trees in a heavy wind; they didn't seem injured, but they didn't seem aware of their surroundings, either.

Boy, I'm not used to this, thought Jim, who until then had never given any value to this so-called Holy Ghost power. Various friends had told him that salvation was just the beginning; that he needed this "deeper walk"; but he had always felt that he had been saved, and anything more was something from long-ago days that didn't exist in modern times. *I want to get out of here,* he thought.

But for some reason he didn't leave. Instead, he began to participate just a little in the singing, and before he knew it he felt a tremendous convulsion in his soul, and he began to sob bitterly. It seemed as though all the hurts and emotions of the past were pouring out of him. He prayed to be set free from his heartaches, from everything that had restricted him and robbed him of the blessings he now knew could be his. He prayed to be allowed to step over that line - to be filled with the Holy Spirit.

Another missionary, Brother Manros, put his hand on Jim's head and prayed for him.

"I could feel some of these old bondages that I'd had in my life for years begin to loosen up and become pliable, and I realized that this is what I was really eager for: a deeper walk in the spirit," Jim said. And then he fell to the floor. He went "under the power," and a glorious joy, a heavenly ecstasy, seemed to fill his soul.

When he finally got up, he spent the rest of the evening dancing in the aisles of the church, rejoicing.

The Duluth revival lasted for many weeks, with many people "going under the spirit"; the energy later flowed over into the little mission at 120 Avenue C. Meetings there began drawing people of all stripes: "respectable" church-goers who parked their cars on a different block so neither their friends nor ministers would know they were attending a skid row mission; rowdy teens; people reeling from drunkenness; evangelists and missionaries and believers from as far as 100 miles away. A spiritual awakening seemed to be taking place. A new brother in this awakening was Jeff Goude, a Christian and construction co-worker who became one of Jim's strongest supports and most faithful friends.

The Filipino team that had prompted this lengthy revival moved on to western North Dakota, to the Fort

Berthold Reservation, home of the Three Affiliated Tribes - Mandan, Hidatsa and Arikara. One evening in early spring, Jim had a feeling that the missionaries were in trouble.

"Those dear people had come thousands of miles to minister to us," Jim said. "And now, suddenly, I just knew that they needed our help." He contacted Jeff, and with two other men dropped everything, and within two hours headed off into the night. They had little money; they hadn't bothered to pack a change of clothing; the car's heater was barely working. Although it was almost Palm Sunday, the weather was still wintry, and the wind wailed icily across the plains.

They arrived at their destination in the early morning. The town was dark and very cold. They knocked on a door. It turned out to be the home of the mayor, who happened to be a Christian. He took them to the place the missionaries were staying, and there were the Filipinos - so very sick that they couldn't even stand up.

"The Enemy had knocked them down, physically," Jim said, referring to the Devil. "And we had been called to minister to them."

The rescuers delivered a combination of prayer, nursing and laying on of hands. The Filipinos revived and were able to get up. The mayor took everyone to his home for food and rest.

The next day the Filipinos were fully recovered, and everyone attended the Assembly of God Palm Sunday services.

There was a little all-Indian chapel nearby, and that evening the visitors went there. The little chapel filled rapidly. Among the parishioners was a woman, Elaine, who was drunk and disorderly. But when she heard the preaching, she suddenly dropped to the floor and began to vomit; as Jim describes it, she was "vomiting up demons." When she rose to her feet she was sober, clear-eyed and prayerful. Then the door opened and a huge figure filled the doorway: Elaine's brother, Nero, who was even more drunk than she had been. He had come to get money from her for a bottle. "Nero, come up here," she called. He walked toward the front; Brother Manros prayed for him; and Nero fell to the floor. When he arose he too was sober; he had been delivered, set free. He strode to the front, picked up a guitar that had been propped against a wall, and began playing and singing "I'll Fly Away."

So this, Jim thought, *is the real reason we have been called here. To help Elaine and Nero.*

The trio left the next day, and much later Jim learned that Nero remained sober, had been reunited with his estranged wife and children, and was living a Christian life.

*   *   *

Back in Cloquet, Jim, Jeff, Joel and others decided to build an actual church. They selected a site several miles into the woods, behind Jim's old home and several miles outside of Cloquet. The

210

sprawling building on Swanson Road had plenty of room for parking.

And they closed the mission at 120 Avenue C.

Jim continued to participate in various prayer circles that met in private houses nearby: at the Mike and Susan Shabaiash home, at the Wicklunds'. At one such gathering, Jim noticed an attractive, petite, dark-haired young woman standing off to the side. He had never seen her here before, and made some inquiries. She was from a large local family, but had been away studying - four years at the College of St. Catherine in St. Paul, plus nine months of field work, most recently in New York City. She was home on a visit before beginning her work as an occupational therapist in the Twin Cities.

Jim had frequently told the girls in his Sunday school class that he was a "confirmed bachelor," but he said so simply to deflect their teenaged interest. He always knew he would get married some day, when he met the right woman; and now, at almost 50 years of age, he suspected he had.

Cheryl Soukkala was only 25, but she was drawn to Jim. "He certainly didn't seem that old," she said. "And I liked his values. He put a high priority on people - as the Lord did."

They began seeing one another; and after a lengthy engagement, Jeff married them in the Swanson Road church. "It was a happy time," Jim said. "A new adventure." The couple honeymooned far up the North Shore of Lake Superior.

Jim's hopes for the Swanson Road church were realized during its first few years of operation. The congregation grew, and, he felt, became united in brotherly love. Visiting evangelists held revivals.

However, as time went on, dissension intruded, and factions arose. Jim hoped to hold it all together by dint of sheer will and rank stubbornness - but it wasn't working. At the same time, he was becoming aware that his days were occupied primarily with the very distractions of the organization he had sought to avoid: building repairs, business meetings, church dinners, the pressures of meeting monthly expenses.

Business meetings? What was all this? Once, he had cut himself off from organized religion. Now he had a mission, all right: a mission *building*, but he was spending less and less time as a missionary. When was the last time he had brought food to a hungry family? Stopped to bring a drunk in out of the cold? Come to think of it, how many poor people, how many alcoholics, could even get out to the church in the woods? It was so far from town - from the marketplace - that you needed a car to get to it. The people he had always ministered to couldn't afford automobiles. How did this happen?

Jim sat down and thought and prayed about it. Snared by churchianity, that's what he was. Many good things had happened here on Swanson Road, but when he looked back on the spiritual richness that had unfolded in the rented skid row storefront at 120 Avenue C, the Swanson Road church felt a little flat.

He decided he'd had it, and he closed the building.

*   *   *

Today, 20 years later, he is reminiscing about that time. We're still in his car, parked in front of the empty storefront at 120 Avenue C.

"We never should have closed this place," he says. "I was never meant to be on a church board, to run an organization, to worry about pews and hymn books. Now I'm back to the simple way: going out where I'm needed, meeting people."

I picture what he has just told me: a church building and a congregation brought together with love and sweat; the large prayer family gradually disintegrating; hopes and dreams toppled; feelings of failure, perhaps of regret. My heart goes out to this man whose heart goes out to everyone.

"Do you ever feel like... well, like you wasted your life?" I ask bluntly. "I mean, you basically sacrificed yourself - living up to the expectations of your mom and grandmother; taking care of them and your dad and your grandfather; rescuing dozens of people like Shirley, cleaning up their messes, paying their bills; helping to raise other people's children...."

Jim thinks hard for awhile. "You know, I never was one of those who doubted God; and I knew that He called me to the mission ministry. Obedience to that 'still small voice' is even greater than salvation.

"It's true there was that control in my family, and it kept me tied down. Once in awhile, I've wondered what my life would have been if I'd gotten out from under it. Lived it differently. Just cut loose and gone my own way.

"But you know, I've had a good life. I wouldn't want it any other way. I wanted to be an ambassador for God - I didn't go to Africa or some other place, and I didn't learn a foreign language; I just stayed at home on the reservation, because the work is right here. Picking up a lunch today for Donnie's son, that's a mission trip. Delivering Roy's finance paperwork from the rez to the prison release program yesterday, that's mission work. Visiting a young man with cancer, and praying with him, like I did yesterday and I'll do again tonight, that's mission work."

"You see? *Every* day is a mission."

*   *   *

Jim's friend Jeff explains, quoting Nehemiah: "'The joy of the Lord is our strength.' That is true for both Jim and me."

Be not forgetful to entertain strangers;
for thereby some have entertained angels unawares.

- Hebrews 13:2

CHAPTER 12

Angels in Disguise

*T*here is an old Jewish legend:
If life is to go on, there must be at least 36 righteous people alive in every generation. No one knows who these *Lamed Vovnikim* are, not even themselves; they are often humble and insignificant. But their great compassion, their suffering for the suffering of others, holds up the world. Lacking even one of them, the world would end.

There is an old Christian legend:
A wealthy man named Julian had committed a great sin; and in shame, he left his riches to do a life of penance as a poor ferryman alongside a river. One cold windy night he heard someone call him from across the river. Braving the waves and cold, he ferried out to pick up the man. When he got him safely across, the man said he had no place to stay, and he was hungry.

Julian took him into his shack and gave him soup and bread. The man said, "I need a bath, but I can't do it by myself." So Julian bathed him; the man's body was covered with weeping sores, and his breath was foul, as though he were rotting inside. Julian helped him get dried and gave him his only nightshirt to wear. The man said, "Give me your bed." So Julian lay on the floor. The man said, "I'm cold." So Julian gave him his own blanket. The man said, "I'm still cold," so Julian climbed in next to the man to warm his dreadful body with his own, ignoring his stinking breath. And then, suddenly, the man was transformed; a radiance shone around him; his sores cleared up; he rose from the bed and stood over Julian, and said, "Blessed Julian, because you gave Me comfort, so too will I comfort you in heaven."

*   *   *

As Jim's grandmother had said so long ago, you should always welcome a stranger into your home, because he or she might be an angel in disguise.

Shirley was no longer a stranger. She had come through their door dozens of times, usually drunk and hollering. But after that early morning deliverance at the old storefront mission at 120 Avenue C, she began to take on the appearance of an angel.

It didn't happen all at once. She was still Shirley - feisty, direct, outspoken, hot-tempered. And although the burdens of alcohol, cigarettes, promiscuity and foul language were gone, she continued to struggle with the attacks of panic that had begun shortly after

Kenny was born. Furthermore, she'd had no practice in how to live a non-alcoholic life, in how to maintain healthy relationships.

She still had a long way to go, but the ground was cleared for her. The unconditional love she had found at the Esalas (which her son Ken later described as "basically buckling her at the knees") had brought her to her point of deliverance; and now she had a place to start, and she started with a determination to make it work.

Ken was almost 30 when Shirley told him she had quit drinking and was starting a new life. "I'd heard that many times before," he said, "So I thought, 'Yeah, yeah.' I mean, her average day was drunk; she'd have an occasional binge of sobriety."

But this time, the "binge of sobriety" continued. As it lengthened, Ken began to wonder if it were true - if the mother he had known all his life really was changed.

"It didn't happen overnight," he said. "There were a lot of skeletons alongside the road; she said things without thinking; she had no tact, verbally or socially.

"But her heart was changed."

Her heart told her to help others.

So she went to Duluth's skid row and, like Jim, began talking to people on the street. This led her to the Union Gospel Mission, a long-established safe harbor for people down on their luck. They came for meals, friendship, encouragement and a place to sleep. The mission was (and continues to be) sponsored by local churches and synagogues.

At first, Shirley was one of many who attended evening services at the old mission. Gradually she took on more responsibility, until the Board of Directors hired her as executive director.

One of her first projects was one for which she had no preparation other than the kind of courageous determination a person acquires when trying to help people one cares about. The mission building, which stood behind where the tribal/city Fond-du-Luth Casino stands today, was condemned by the city. There was no money for another.

Shirley sat inside the building, scowling in deep thought as she watched her clients - her friends - read the "closed" sign on the door and wander away again. Finally she slapped her hands on the table, jumped to her feet, grabbed her purse and marched down the street, to the door of Minnesota Power, a Duluth-based power company serving northern Minnesota. She shoved open the door and barreled up to the receptionist.

"I want to see the guy who runs this place," she demanded.

While she waited, fidgeting, trying to head off an anxiety attack, she reminded herself that most people are caring and genuine. She cared about her mission friends; the Esalas had cared about her. Why wouldn't wealthy people in a big fancy building care about poor people at the mission? Of course they would.

A half hour later, when she was ushered into the CEO's office, she felt calmer and certain of success. She settled into a chair and explained to the CEO about the mission and the condemnation.

"At first we got condemned just because of the wiring, and I figured that since they're more or less your wires because it's your electricity that goes through, you should've had them in good shape for the people who need the mission, who really need it, and you probably have a lot more money than you need. So now the problem is much worse, and I hope you can fix our problem."

The CEO stared at her: a short, round little woman, obviously with some hard years behind her, cheaply dressed but very clean, red-faced and freckled, shoulder-length badly barbered hair, wearing eyeglasses and sneakers, apparently poorly educated - sitting here with her jaw out and her teeth clenched like a little bulldog, making demands on one of the biggest corporations in the upper Midwest.

He smiled. "I'll see what I can do."

Three days later, Minnesota Power found another building to house the Union Gospel Mission. The company took the lead on getting corporate commitments for expensive renovations, and directly donated $40,000 for a new kitchen. In a short time, the mission was open again - not far from the old place, still on skid row, but this time with a sunny southern exposure.

"Way to go, Shirley!" the diners called across the table during the first meal in the new mission.

"It's good to be all together again," she said.

*   *   *

Taking her cue from the Esalas, Shirley didn't preach at people and she wasn't shy about directly challenging them - although her style was more "in your face" than her mentors'.

"Hey Fred!" she yelled across the mission's dining tables to a man who was whining loudly about not having a job and being unlucky in love. "If you'd shave once in a while and stop swearing all the time, maybe you'd do better in a job interview, and maybe somebody would go on a date with you!"

Fred glowered at her and told her to get off his case. But later, when she brought him an unopened packet of plastic razors, a new can of shaving foam and an almost-new, freshly ironed blue shirt, she got a big smile.

"You're a queen, Shirley, a f- — I mean, you're one in a million, Shirley."

"Don't I know it. So are you."

Roger wasn't so sure he liked the woman his wife was becoming. All her energy went into the mission. "I liked you better when you were drinking," he growled. Nevertheless, he went along with her when she moved into a room above the mission. He began working there as a janitor, cook and all-around helper. Because he was also a drunk who occasionally was disorderly out on the street, it made for a complicated relationship with his wife-supervisor. The couple was drifting apart.

Shirley wasn't the kind of director who stayed in her office and delegated tasks. She spent most of her time interacting with people in the mission, and walking the bowery streets. She would stride up to people on the corner and befriend or confront them, and tell them they had to get their life in order.

"What do you mean?" Heather, an obese, scantily-dressed young prostitute, asked in alarm.

"Don't you want a better quality of life?"

Well, sure. Everybody wants that.

"Then you get started by getting cleaned up." She meant it literally: Wash your face, change your underwear, quit swearing, dress with self-respect, eat right, get a good night's sleep. "Then we can work on some of those other problems that I know you've got, like not liking yourself and being fat and maybe having clap. God will help us, if you want Him to. If you don't, we'll work on them anyhow, together."

Later, Shirley thought about her advice to Heather. How could the girl dress with self-respect when she had no money for clothes, except what she earned by dressing with self-disrespect? Clothes were an ongoing problem for all of her mission clients.

So Shirley hunted up an empty old building nearby, wheedled a low rent out of the owner, and asked the churches and synagogues to do a clothing drive. Before long, the thrift shop was filled with clothing, staffed by two full-time employees - mission regulars - and turning a small profit.

Sometimes Shirley would run into one of her old boyfriends or drinking partners, who would remind her of her old peccadilloes.

"Yeah, I was a drunk," she freely admitted. Self-righteousness was never one of her faults. "But I found a different way to live, and I'm happy."

"How did that happen?"

"I found the father I was always looking for: my Heavenly Father."

*   *   *

Ken often dropped in at the mission to see how his mother was doing.

"Do you have to be anywhere for the next couple of hours?" Shirley asked one day.

"No, not really." He did, but he liked seeing her at work, and he knew she felt happy when he was around.

"I've been working with some people who are hanging out down by the lake, on the rocks behind Fitger's. Want to go down there with me today?"

"Okay."

They descended the hill to the old brewery, empty now for a decade, and circled behind it and down the rocks toward Lake Superior. The freeway that would pass below a renovated Fitger's had not yet been built. They pushed their way through some brush. It was a warm summer afternoon.

"Mom, this is pretty tough going, and I'm wearing my best slacks and shoes," Ken objected.

"We're almost there."

Finally they came to a little clearing. Two Indian men jumped to their feet, startled. Shirley was wearing a mission badge, and Ken figured they were wary of any kind of badge that had an official look. Behind them was a lean-to, assembled from old boards and cardboard, which contained a couple of blankets and some clothing. A third person sleepily arose from the blankets.

"Oh, it's Shirley!" the tallest man said. Everyone relaxed; smiles and laughter all around.

"How goes it, Shirl?"

"We haven't seen you for awhile."

"Are you hungry?"

Ken saw two freshly opened cans of baked beans and several spoons balanced on a rock.

His mother introduced him; he recognized one man as a cousin of a friend from Cloquet, and they visited about old times as they shared some beans. Then Shirley got down to business.

"How are you guys doing?"

"Oh fine, fine."

"No, I mean how are you guys *really* doing?"

The smiles vanished.

"Well, at least it's summer," one man said.

"Are you getting enough food?"

They gestured toward the beans.

"Why don't you come up to the mission to eat?"

"It's nice down here by the lake. And, you know, all the bars up there - it's hard to get away again."

Shirley frowned. "Is that the only reason? Anybody having trouble walking? What about you, Eugene, are your feet okay?"

Eugene was the sleepy one. He didn't answer.

One of the other men caught Shirley's eye. He shook his head and pursed his lips toward Eugene's left foot.

"Lemme see your foot."

"Naw, you don't want to do that, Shirley," Eugene roused himself, smiling and blushing. "My feet are a mite stinky. I don't even want to look at them."

"You can't be that way, Eugene," she scolded. "You got to check your feet every day. And keep them clean. Here, you got the biggest lake in the world a few feet away, and you aren't even washing your feet? C'mon! Just 'cause you're a diabetic and a drunk and the water is like ice, that don't mean you can't wash!"

Everybody laughed, and Shirley began unlacing the shoe. When she peeled the sweaty sock off, she drew back with a worried look. A pressure sore was suppurating below the inside ankle, and a red line extended several inches up the leg.

Eugene looked apologetic. "I don't have any other socks, so what's the point of washing my feet?"

"Couldn't you wash the socks?"

"Seems like I'm too tired to do anything."

"I s'pose you're out of insulin."

"No, I've still got a little. But I'm out of syringes. And even if I did have some, I can't test my blood; the strips got rained on and spoiled."

Shirley took off the other shoe and sock, checked that foot, and handed both socks to the taller man. "You go wash these, Hank, and lay them out on a rock in the sun to dry. Squeeze them good first, and turn them over a couple of times, because they got to be dry in three hours. That's when you and Floyd got to get Eugene up to the street, because Roger's going to be there with the mission van to take him to the hospital."

Hank nodded. "I would've washed the socks before, Shirley, but Eugene, he never asked me to, and I never thought of it."

"That's okay. Just make sure you get him up to the street."

As she rose to her feet to go, the third man, Floyd, stopped her. "Shirl, you take care of teeth as well as feet?"

"Why?"

"I got a hell of a toothache."

"Why don't you come to the mission after you get Eugene set, and I'll fix you up with a voucher for a dentist?"

"Okay. Sure. Thanks."

*　　*　　*

The telephone rang at Ken's house.

"Ken, we're having a board meeting tonight and I want you to come help me out," his mother's panicky voice shrilled.

"Calm down, Mom. What's going on?"

"One of the board members said they're giving me a $50 raise because I'm working so hard, and I don't want it."

Shirley's pay was $600 a month, plus the upstairs room.

"I don't understand. What's $50? You deserve it."

"Well I don't want it, and I'll quit if they make me take it. I need you here."

Representatives of several dozen churches and synagogues sat on the mission board; about 15 people were at the meeting. The chairman talked about the good work Shirley had been doing; the phenomenal growth in the mission outreach; the jump in monthly donations. He concluded with the announcement that Shirley would be given a raise.

Shirley glanced at Ken, took a deep breath, and jumped to her feet.

"I'm personally insulted by this," she said. "You guys take up special offerings, and you come here and serve soup and sandwiches; you know the need is growing all the time. I don't need this raise; the people we are helping are the ones that need it."

"But Shirley, we want to show you our appreciation; we certainly aren't trying to insult you!"

Shirley looked stubborn. "If this mission ever gets to the point where people are doing this for a real job, we should close the front doors. If you give me this raise, I'm out of here."

The board members appeared flabbergasted, but Ken could sense the esteem in which they held his mother. His heart swelled in pride. "We should all be like her," he thought.

*   *   *

Roger's heavy drinking was not only a strain on their relationship, but on Shirley's relationship with the board. Finally the two became so estranged that they got a divorce.

Not long afterwards, Shirley fell ill. The diagnosis was melanoma, which had spread throughout her body; the doctors guessed she had six months to live. Since there was no treatment, she remained at home. Ken visited her often and called her daily.

"I want you to forgive me, Kenny," she told her son one day, reaching for his hand.

"For what, Mom?"

"For what? For everything. For taking away your dream of football - "

"I forgave you for that a long time ago," Ken interrupted. It was true, too. "I gave it up out of love - love for you, and I don't regret it."

Shirley began to cry. "Oh Kenny, thank you, but I'm so sorry, I'm so sorry for not being a mother all those years, for leaving you all alone, day after day, night after night, month after month...year after year." She was sobbing now.

Ken's eyes filled with tears too. "Mom, I always knew you cared."

She wiped her eyes. "How could you know that, the way I acted?"

"You wouldn't believe me if I told you."

Shirley sniffed. "Try me."

Ken looked at his mother's little hand, resting in his. The tears that had pooled in his eyes spilled down his cheeks. "You remember how you always used to leave me notes?"

She nodded.

"That's why. You never forgot to leave me a note and a little money for a hamburger. And you tried to come back when the note said you would."

She snorted. "That's pitiful. What a way to be a mother."

"No, it was a big thing. See, I understood at a very young age that you were sick. I knew you wanted to be with me, that you felt connected to me, but you couldn't stay. You wouldn't have left a note if you hadn't felt connected. And that made all the difference. You weren't leaving me because you didn't care; you were leaving me because you were sick."

Shirley nodded. "That was how it was," she whispered. She squeezed his hand. "And that's how it is now, too."

Shirley died that night. Ken called his dad with the news, and Roger went on a bender that kept him drunk until after the funeral.

*　　*　　*

Shirley had left Ken instructions to have her funeral at the mission. However, he didn't want his own mother's funeral to take place in a bowery building where drunks hung out. It was embarrassing; it wasn't dignified. He was making other arrangements when his wife talked him into honoring his mother's wishes. As it turned out, the decision was right.

A stunning array of people came to honor the late Shirley Johnson. There wasn't even standing room in the mission, which was crammed with 500 people from all walks of life. Jim Esala, of course; the mayors of Duluth and Superior; business people; community leaders. And street people: all cleaned up, wearing dresses and suits and ties they had picked up at the thrift store with mission vouchers. One-legged Eugene, wearing a suit and a prosthesis.

Clean-shaven Fred. Heather, wearing a modest but becoming dress.

Ken realized that none of the mission clients would have been likely to come to Shirley's funeral if it had been held in a funeral home or traditional church. He felt grateful to his wife for insisting on honoring his mother's wishes.

After the service, after everyone had come up to him conveying their condolences, Shirley's mission clients remained. Their acute grief showed Ken what a light his mother had been for many of them. It wasn't about religion - that was in her back pocket, all right, but it was mainly about hope. His mother, a drunk for most of her life, panic-struck and uneducated, had offered them - no, *given* them - hope. She had done it the same way Jim had helped her: By being absolutely faithful in accepting them, always, no matter what. No matter if they were stinky or drunk or unkind; no matter if they had sexually transmitted diseases or a criminal past; no matter if they swore or conned her or used drugs.

As he stood there, still stunned and trying to understand his mother's impact on all these lives, he noticed a man whom people called Boxcar Willie standing over in the corner. Willie was a railroad bum who came to the mission whenever his train was in town. His mother was good friends with him, although Willie was mistrustful of most people and otherwise uncommunicative. Usually he wore a long grey beard and cast-off clothes, but today he was clean-shaven and wearing a three-piece suit. It took a moment for Ken to recognize him.

"How are you doing?" Ken asked.

"Not so good," Willie mumbled.

"Well, you sure look good."

"I don't feel comfortable. But I did this for your mother."

*   *   *

Long before this chapter was written, Jim's "brother," Don Hanson, sent an email. "I hope this isn't meddling in your book," he wrote, "but maybe this will be of some help in understanding what happened to Shirley."

He quoted several passages from the Apostle Paul's second letter to the Corinthians: that those who are "in Christ" become a new creation, and then they become ambassadors for Christ.

"That is what Shirley became," Don's email concluded. "An official representative of God."

When people turn their thoughts to the Creator,
they give the Creator power to enter their minds
and to bring good thoughts.

- Tadodaho Leon Shenandoah

CHAPTER 13

Every Day is a Mission

Jim woke up early, as was his habit. He stretched. His 77-year-old muscles were only a little achy. Lying there in bed, he thought of his "visit" of a few hours earlier.

For years now, Jim had been awaking at 3 o'clock most mornings, and in that quiet hour, he had a prayerful closeness to God. He called it "visiting with my Father." His friends began calling these visits "divine appointments," because Jim was given inspirational direction for the next day - the names of people who needed spiritual companionship, simple company or material help. Not that there was a holy voice telling him, "Go see So-and-So at noon today"; rather, there was a deep tranquility, and into it came a clear thought of someone - a divine message.

This morning, four people were on his list. The first was Ken's dad, Roger Johnson. Roger had always been a hard case. That long-ago dramatic change in Shirley's life hadn't affected Roger much; he remained a stubborn man whose main obstacle was pride. In addition, he was seriously addicted to nicotine. In fact, his primary activity was smoking one cigarette after another - as though somewhere in the home Ken had bought for him there existed a huge pile of cigarettes that he was required to go through before he died.

After Jim drove Chery to work, he dropped by Roger's. He stepped out of the bright sunshine into Roger's living room, made dim by sagging drapes, nicotine-fogged windows and unreflecting smoke-stained walls. A painting of Ken and his family hung crookedly on one wall. Their smiling faces were the only obvious bright spot in the room. But Jim's focus was on the bright spot deep inside the collapsed man sitting before him.

"Hello there, Roger!" Jim greeted him in his buoyant cheerful way.

"Yeah. Hi. C'mon in." His voice was smoke-ragged; he gasped for each breath.

Roger had reduced his living quarters to this living room. He had moved his bed in there, where he could do his smoking day and night. Three ashtrays were overflowing.

They chatted for awhile about the weather and Ken and his family, and then got around to mutual acquaintances.

"Remember the fella they used to call Samson?" Jim asked. "The salesman whose drinking put him out of business?

Roger dragged on his cigarette, and went into a coughing fit. Finally, gasping, he said, "Yeah, I remember him. He used to live with what's-her-name. The woman down on the Island."

"Janet. They're still together. Well, Roger, I think the Lord is moving in their lives."

Roger just looked at him, his chest heaving as he breathed.

"I felt a burden yesterday to stop in and see them." Actually, Jim had been given another "divine appointment," but there was no point in mentioning that to Roger. "So I did. And here, they were having a crisis. Samson's son had been in a bad accident and they had no way of getting to Duluth, to the hospital. They were genuinely happy to see me; asked me in to dinner, and we prayed together before I drove them into town."

"I suppose you gave them money too."

"Well, they were pretty hard up. I gave them what I had. It wasn't much."

"Hmmmh. You drive a couple of winos all the way to Duluth and you give them money. You were being conned."

Jim smiled. "Maybe they did think they were trying to con me, but that's not my affair. I was just doing what the Lord led me to do. They didn't twist my arm or anything."

"Hah. You've always been a con man's dream. The cons ask you for money, and you give it. Ask you for a ride, and you give it. Tell you they love Jesus, and you believe them."

"Why not? Why not give people money who need it? How do I know there isn't something moving inside them, bringing them to Jesus? If I was going to say, "I don't believe that you love Jesus,' would that bring them closer to the Lord?"

Roger's lip curled. "You just don't get it, do you?"

Jim smiled again. "Maybe not. But let me tell you a story. About 10 years ago, this fellow, he was a neighbor, a very rough man, a murderer who'd been in and out of prison a couple of times - "

"Indian guy?" Roger interrupted. "Yeah, I know who you mean. Charlie what's-his-name."

"That's him. He used to come over every so often - called my mother 'Ma.' Sometimes he'd bring a few friends and ask Mom to play the organ and sing gospel songs. Other times he came for a meal - she liked to feed him, and he sure liked her cooking. He always put on a show about the Lord. I guess he figured he wouldn't get fed without a show. Oh, I knew he didn't know the Word, and I knew he thought he didn't want to know it. But that didn't matter. He was precious in God's eyes, and if God loves him, who am I to feel different?

"Anyway, I had done something for him, I don't remember what, and he said, 'Jim, I'm not just a taker. I'm going to bring you over a nice chicken for roasting.' Well, I didn't expect him to, and he didn't. But many weeks later came a knock on the door. There he was, drunk. He held out a little plastic bag, and there was a chicken neck in it.

"You see, he hadn't forgotten. He fulfilled his promise."

Roger snorted. "There you go! A chicken neck? The guy was insulting you, and you don't even know it! You take it like some damn sign you're getting through to him!"

"It wasn't me getting through to him; it was the Lord. Oh, I could look at it like it was an insult. If I did, that would have done nothing but harden his heart, and maybe mine too. But look at it this way: He still was thinking about it all. He made some kind of effort to make a connection. A seed had been planted...the human heart yearns for closeness to God, and he didn't know how to go about it. That was the best he could do just then."

They were silent awhile. Roger's chest heaved with his laborious breathing. Then Jim asked, "Would you like us to pray, Roger?"

"I don't need you to pray," Roger growled. "I'm an ordained minister, did you forget?" He gestured toward a framed mail-order ministry certificate on the wall. It had cost him $15 and two stamps.

"No, I didn't forget. Would you like to lead us in prayer?"

"Not now. Maybe next time."

Out on the street, Jim took a deep breath of fresh air and looked up into the trees across from Roger's house. They were just beginning to change color; there was a snap of fall in the air. He loved this time of year. *What a blessing,* he thought, *to be able to breathe. To be able to smell this good smell. Thank you, Lord.*

He said a prayer for Roger: that he too could experience the gift of unobstructed breath - and the greater gift of unobstructed intimacy with God.

*　　*　　*

The next person on his "divine appointment" list was Sharon, a defense attorney married to a general contractor who was the roughest, toughest man Jim had met in all his years in the mission ministry. Kurt seemed to hate everybody: women, Indians, Blacks, Jews, foreigners, poor people, unions, lawyers. He was abusively opinionated and sarcastic to everyone, and he had battered Sharon both physically and verbally for most of their 19-year marriage. A few months earlier, a serious on-site accident put him in the hospital; Sharon quickly availed herself of that window of safety to obtain a protection order against him and begin divorce proceedings.

Jim had tried to talk her out of the divorce; he told her that in God's eyes, marriage is a lifetime covenant commitment, and God holds us to that commitment; divorce is displeasing to Him. Sharon had been furious with him. Privately, he could scarcely blame her for pursuing a divorce; even to Jim, Kurt's deadly combination of anger and abundant money sometimes made him seem like a hopeless case.

But something had happened to the man since his accident. When Jim visited him in the hospital, Kurt's aggressive arrogance was gone. He expressed regret and shame for driving Sharon to such extremities, and seemed genuinely sorry for her pain. Jim sensed that his regret was deep, and, with support, could be lasting. They had prayed together, and when Kurt was released from the hospital, he began accompanying Jim to local Bible studies. People who knew the contractor were amazed at the change in him.

Today, Jim wondered whether Sharon was aware of the changes happening in Kurt, and whether she would care. As he climbed the steps of the luxurious Duluth home, a dog barked. "Hush, Molly!" Sharon's voice rang out, and then she opened the door. Her face lit up. "Jim! Come in!"

Molly, a Labrador mix, wagged alongside him, licking his hand and nudging him into a ficus tree in the airy entryway.

"I'm so glad to see you!" Sharon bubbled as they settled into upholstered chairs in the living room. "This is an amazing coincidence! I was hoping you'd come today."

She looked very different. Jim had known Sharon for years, because some of her public-defender clients were part of his mission circle; and she usually wore a hang-dog look, even when she was dressed for the office. Now she appeared younger somehow, and stronger, and happier than he'd ever seen her. He reluctantly acknowledged to himself that the separation from Kurt must be doing her good.

"You'll never guess what happened," she said, and then without waiting for his response, continued, "I stopped the divorce proceedings. I've filed for legal separation instead."

Jim raised his eyebrows. "Well! That is good!"

"I was so mad at you, you and your Christian preaching, when you wouldn't give me your approval about the divorce - I don't know why I wanted your approval, anyway...."

"Neither do I. My opinions don't matter."

"But you were right. I married Kurt for better or worse. And I'm pretty sure that the worst is over. I've never seen him like this - he's really changed."

"You've seen him? I thought he couldn't come near you."

"Yes, well, I had the protection order lifted too. He's living on the next block. I want the legal separation just in case he - what do you guys call it? - going backwards?"

"Backslides."

"That's it. I'm hedging my bets. I'm definitely not going to stay with a man who pounds on me and makes me feel like I'm crap and could kill me, and I can't believe that God would want me to.

"But Jim, I think he's - we're - going to make it. It's a miracle, and you're a big part of making it happen." She stopped and looked down at her hands. "I'm sorry I dumped on you before, when I was mad at you."

Jim smiled. "Sharon, we all go through these things in life. I've dumped on my friends; we dump on each other when we have problems, but we're friends, and we pray together. That's what friends are for."

Sharon nodded.

"Kurt needs love now, and we've got to stand with him," Jim counseled. "And he's going to make it!"

Sharon nodded again, vigorously this time, and then laughed out loud. "Get this: He's going to ask your group to have your next Bible study at his apartment, and I'm making the refreshments!"

How about that, Jim thought as he drove down the steep hill and onto the freeway. *A family reuniting. Love triumphant.* Then he added aloud, "Hallelujah! Thank you, Jesus!"

*   *   *

Jim's third "divine appointment" was with Reino Mikkonen. He hadn't seen the old heathen for several months now. As he swung down Reino's dirt lane outside of Cloquet, he could see Reino splitting wood; about a cord was already piled to one side.

"It's the wrong day to visit me, Jim," Reino growled. "I'm just primed to take a swing at one of you goddamn Christians, and even though I like you personally, you're the only one available."

Jim picked up an armload of wood and began stacking it. "What's wrong?"

Reino split another dozen sticks furiously. He stopped and turned to Jim.

"Who do you hate?"

"Me? Nobody."

"Bullshit. You'd be right in the middle of *Kristallnacht* if you lived back then."

"Crystal - what?"

"Never mind. I forgot you don't pay much attention to unimportant things like history and politics."

Jim ignored Reino's taunting sarcasm. "What's wrong, Reino?"

"Aaaah, this damn preacher over here, he stopped me downtown today. Little Joey was with me - you know, my great-grandson? You know his mom is Jewish? Anyway, this preacher said he felt an evil presence, that's what he called it, in his church at a wedding on Saturday, and he later found out - he actually said this - 'Jews! I found out there were Jews in the congregation!' That's what he said, and he looked right at Joey when he said it. Man, I wanted to tear him apart right there."

Jim kept piling wood.

"How does anybody in the twenty-first century get so damn dumb, and so mean, and so, so - do they teach you guys how to be stupid and vicious in your Sunday schools? How do you get that way?"

Jim was silent.

Reino glared at him. "You can't answer that, can you?"

"No, I can't. I don't know the answers. I know why people can be cruel, though...."

"Oh yeah, blame the Devil," Reino interrupted. "That's a good excuse."

"Well, what other explanation is there? Where does evil come from? You don't think God made it, do you?"

Reino tossed his axe aside and began piling wood. "Now you're trying to trip me up with your kind of logic. I'm too mad to be logical. Anyway, I don't have any answers either. All I know is, I wish those narrow-minded, ignorant SOBs would drop through a hole in the ground and –"

"Burn in hell?"

"Yeah, that'd be good. You want a sandwich?"

"Yeah, that'd be good."

They walked toward the house.

"And Jim," Reino said, "I don't really think you'd be part of *Kristallnacht*. Fact is, I know you wouldn't."

"Thanks. I guess."

*   *   *

The final divine appointment was with a man who lived out near Cromwell; Jim had met him in a recent prayer group. His place was 30 miles on the other side of Cloquet.

He checked his gas gauge. Just about on Empty, the same as his wallet. Well, if the Lord wanted him to visit Douglas, the Lord would take care of the gas. He drove down the Big Lake Road and turned west onto Highway 210 toward Cromwell.

Douglas was about 55, a twice-divorced Vietnam vet who made his living in a hodgepodge of jobs - cutting pulpwood, a little farming, a little trucking. Jim had heard that Douglas had a couple of estranged kids and a drug problem. His place was out in the country.

The gas gauge showed a little below Empty when Jim pulled into the driveway. A cluster of vehicles was in the yard - an ATV, a Chev pickup, a lumber truck, a Suburban, a John Deere tractor, and, under wraps until the snow flew, an Arctic Cat snow machine. Flashing light, probably from a welder, made the garage windows appear to be blinking.

Jim knocked on the garage door. The blinking stopped and the door was wrenched open. An intense, angry-looking man wearing a tipped-back welding mask gave him an appraising, suspicious look.

"Douglas? Jim Esala - we met last week over at Henderson's," Jim said pleasantly, extending his hand.

Douglas reluctantly pulled off one welding glove and shook Jim's hand. He motioned him inside. "Yeah, I remember you."

A radio was playing - one of the AM talk shows. The garage was full of expensive-looking equipment, and its walls were lined with tools, mostly for auto repair, neatly arranged by size and function.

"You do mechanic work?"

"Some." Douglas kept the welding mask balanced on his head, as though willing this to be a very short visit.

Jim examined the welding project. "Looks like a frame of some sort. Trailer?"

"For the snow machine," Douglas said.

Jim inspected the welds. "You do good work."

"Thanks."

They talked about snow and trailers and the people at the previous week's prayer meeting.

"How did you happen to go to the meeting?" Jim asked. "You didn't say."

"Nothin' better to do that night," Douglas replied. "I probably won't go back." He sighed and took off his welding mask. He placed it on the table near the radio, just as a newscaster was saying something about torture at the Guantanamo and Abu Ghraib prisons. He glared at the radio. "All that fuss about what they call torture," he said. "What do they think war is? We got to get information from our enemies if we're going to protect ourselves. Some of these anti-war wimps..."

Douglas awaited Jim's comment, but Jim was silent.

"It says right in the Bible, that we got to wipe out our enemies," Douglas added.

"Where does it say that?"

"One of the Old Testament books. God told the Jews to kill ALL their enemies, even their cattle."

Jim was quiet. He had heard this argument before, on the radio, and it seemed to be catching on. He was often struck by the way some believers seemed to miss the whole idea of the new covenant God had made, through Jesus.

"They call it torture," Douglas continued with a scoffing tone. "A little sexual stuff that makes those Moslems embarrassed because of their weird culture. That's not torture."

"So do you think it's something Jesus would approve of?"

Douglas frowned. "That's not the point. We got to win, don't we? If people aren't our friends, then they're our enemies. And if they're enemies, we got to beat them. We got to survive."

"What if winning and surviving aren't our purpose in life?"

Douglas blinked a couple of times. "I don't get you."

"What if our purpose in life is to find intimacy with the Lord?"

Douglas was silent.

"Jesus said we should love our enemies."

"Well, yeah, but if love doesn't work, and they want to kill you, you better get them first. Besides, you can't love these fanatics. You show them love, and they'll cream you. They don't think like we do. Their religion teaches them to kill people."

The younger man seemed unaware of the irony of his last comment; he was consumed in tension. Rage, or maybe outrage, seemed to bubble inside him.

"I don't think the Lord made any exceptions," Jim said. "He just said we should love our enemies. He told us to bless them and do good to them and pray for them."

Douglas shook his head. "Nope. People like that - they'll just take advantage. You act forgiving, they'll use it against you. They use our Christianity against us all the time."

"Do they scare you?"

"Who, me? No! I'm saved - it don't matter to me, I know where I'm going. We're at the Endtime; let them blow everything up, I'll be taken right up to Heaven."

Jim was silent, and let the silence lengthen.

The silence seemed to make Douglas nervous, and he eventually broke it. "So what do you think?"

Jim thought carefully before he answered. "Well I'll tell you, Douglas, it's really sad what's going on in the world today - so much tragedy. I agree with you that this is probably the Endtime. The Bible tells us that in the Endtime there will be false prophets, and even Christians"- he looked directly into Douglas' eyes - "*saved* Christians, could fall from the Truth. People are gullible; we fall into line. We listen to the false teachings, and err, and fall. So we have to be as wise as a serpent and harmless as a dove."

He picked up a rag from the floor and draped it over a bench. "I don't believe in torture, whether its wartime or not," he continued. "I saw some of that abuse on the islands in the Pacific - the attitude and language of Americans toward the Japanese POWs - and the Japanese were just victims too."

"The Goo- the Japs were our enemies!"

"Sure, but we're supposed to love our enemies. We're supposed to have compassion for the enemy."

Douglas' face was losing its stern expression. Uncertainty was taking its place.

Jim gently put his hand on Douglas' shoulder. "When we're in the military, we're trained to kill. That's what we were taught - who the enemy is, and to do away with him. But that's not what the Lord put in the hearts of young people. So, in war, when young soldiers do devastating things, it goes against them deep down. They just break."

Douglas quickly turned away as though to get more welding rod. Jim walked over to the window. He could see part of Corona Bog from here. The peatland was peaceful. There were no soldiers, no tanks, no bombs, no blasted bodies. But even here there was pain. He could feel it throbbing in the garage.

"The Lord heals all wounds, Douglas," he said, still looking out the window. "No sin is too great for Him."

Sometimes Jim's "divine appointment" visits were simply sociable. Sometimes they prompted two or three more visits, which not infrequently ended in spiritual enrichment. Sometimes, like that afternoon, they resulted in an immediate and profound change in a hurting person. Right on the greasy garage floor, Douglas knelt with Jim, prayed with him, and became a different man.

Late that night, after goodbyes and as Jim was starting his car, Douglas called, "Wait a minute, Jim!" and walked over to the elevated gas tank on the other side of the driveway. "Why don't you pull your car over here, and let me gas it up for you."

...Faith and humility are inseparable. In perfect humility all selfishness disappears and your soul no longer lives for itself... it is lost and submerged in Him and transformed into Him.

– Thomas Merton

EPILOGUE

We Can All be Finders of Shirleys

In the many months I have known Jim Esala, I have been struck by his utter peace and his absence of judgment. He has never asked me about my religious upbringing or spiritual beliefs or ethnicity. He has never asked me about my politics, or my thoughts on global warming or evolution or abortion or homosexuality.

In part, he might have been helping me to maintain a wall of objectivity between writer and subject. But mostly, I think, Jim is not much interested in what is in our heads. He's interested in what's in our hearts. And he simply wants to be who he is: a man who lives in intimacy with and obedience to God. If he follows that straight and narrow path, he believes, the goodness from God will flow through him and touch others.

That flow is important, because the Great Commandments - to love God and to love our neighbors - are what Jim is all about.

I saw anger flare in his eyes only once, and that was when he made a disparaging remark about the American Civil Liberties Union. I flinched. I am a card-carrying ACLU member, and one of 11 who signed onto an ACLU lawsuit to get the Ten Commandments removed from the lawn in front of City Hall in Duluth. The lawsuit left something of a storm in its wake, with public protests and Ten Commandments signs appearing in yards throughout the region.

In the interests of that wall of objectivity, I decided to wait until the book was completed before telling Jim of my ACLU connection. I didn't fear his criticism, because that isn't his way. I suppose the anger in his eyes could have made me wonder again whether I had made a mistake in taking on the book - whether after all, he was just some hard-nosed fanatic. But I already knew enough about Jim to know that he isn't like that. Consequently, his anger made me want to see the ACLU from his perspective. I continue to support and greatly value the ACLU, but I no longer see its opponents as somehow un-American or wrongheaded or anti-democratic.

To me, Jim is actually the embodiment of what the ACLU is all about: protection of an individual's rights against majority rule, when (as the joke goes), two wolves and a sheep vote on what's for dinner. Jim lives his life and worships in his own way, regardless of what other Christians, church organizations, and non-Christians say is true or proper. Probably some Americans would just as soon pass a law that would silence him and everyone like him. After all, if everybody followed Jim's path, who would buy all that stuff in the malls? Who would build ostentatious, wildlife-killing, resource-gobbling monster mansions? Who would teach the art of torture in Georgia?

Jim has gone his own way his whole life, following the path that only he can say is the one meant for him. He helps others on his own; he has no certification, no sponsorship, no liability insurance; he writes no grants; he just does it, one human being helping another. He discovered that path through prayer, through his own personal and direct connection with God. He rejects the idea that a particular person or group has the right to meddle with that connection, or to usurp anyone's potential role as ambassador of the Lord. That's the only role that matters, according to Jim, and it's a role that is available to each and every one of us. We can all be finders of Shirleys.

As a former reporter, I know that people can get extraordinarily touchy about being quoted or described, as though their words and experiences are pearls that mustn't be blemished by any paraphrasing or interpretation. Not Jim. He read some chapters before the book went to print, and he had no problem with any of it. It was as though he had no ego. More than anything else, it was this response that showed me his remarkable humility.

This whole writing journey has been an opportunity to look through the eyes of an independent evangelical Christian, someone who has been generous and trusting about letting me use his eyes. I hope I haven't betrayed that trust.

Susan Stanich
Fond du Lac
Duluth, Minnesota
March, 2007

Message to readers from Jim and Don

If this story about a man who lived with genuine compassion has touched your life, and you want to get in touch with Jim or others, you are welcome to contact our website: www.29thavenuepress.com.

If you don't have a computer or don't know how to use one, go to the library and ask them to help you find this website.

It does not matter to God whether you have been lower than Shirley or are sitting on top of the world. You may have fame, power and all the money in the world, but you still may be empty inside and need help and answers. The first step you need to take is to call out to Jesus in prayer. Prayer is simply talking to God. Whatever you say to Him will not be a surprise to Him, because he knows everything about you. More importantly, He still loves you.

The second step you can take is to get in contact with us through our website. We will need to know how to reach you, either by telephone, email, letter or even, if possible, we will try to contact you in person. We really are sincere about finding and helping the Shirleys in this world. Remember, it does not matter how bad you've been, or how far from God you have gone; Jesus loves you and still wants to set you free from everything that has held you captive.

To order copies of *Finding Shirley*, contact:

29th Avenue Press

P.O. Box 16047
Duluth, MN 55816-0047

www.29thavenuepress.com

CPSIA information can be obtained at www.ICGtesting.com
Printed in the USA
BVOW041635080512

289630BV00001BA/2/A